MW00851119

Hellmira

THE UNION'S MOST INFAMOUS CIVIL WAR PRISON CAMP–ELMIRA, NY

by Derek Maxfield

EMERGING CIVIL WAR SERIES

Chris Mackowski, series editor
Chris Kolakowski, chief historian

The Emerging Civil War Series

offers compelling, easy-to-read overviews of some of the Civil War's most important battles and stories.

Recipient of the Army Historical Foundation's Lieutenant General Richard G. Trefry Award for contributions to the literature on the history of the U.S. Army

Also part of the Emerging Civil War Series:

Aftermath of Battle: The Burial of the Civil War Dead
   by Meg Groeling

All Hell Can't Stop Them: The Battles for Chattanooga: Missionary Ridge and Ringgold, November 24-27, 1863
   by David A. Powell

Attack at Daylight and Whip Them: The Battle of Shiloh, April 6-7, 1862
   by Gregory A. Mertz

Battle Above the Clouds: Lifting the Siege of Chattanooga and the Battle of Lookout Mountain, October 16-November 24, 1863
   by David A. Powell

Call Out the Cadets: The Battle of New Market, May 15, 1864
   By Sarah Kay Bierle

Grant's Last Battle: The Story Behind the Personal Memoirs of Ulysses S. Grant
   by Chris Mackowski

The Great Battle Never Fought: The Mine Run Campaign, November 26-December 2, 1863
   by Chris Mackowski

Let Us Die Like Men: The Battle of Franklin, November 30, 1864
   By William Lee White

The Most Desperate Acts of Gallantry: George A. Custer in the Civil War
   By Daniel T. Davis

A Want of Vigilance: The Bristoe Station Campaign, October 9-19, 1863
   by Bill Backus and Rob Orrison

For a complete list of titles in the Emerging Civil War Series, visit www.emergingcivilwar.com.

Hellmira

THE UNION'S MOST INFAMOUS
CIVIL WAR PRISON CAMP–ELMIRA, NY

by Derek Maxfield

EMERGING CIVIL WAR SERIES

SB

Savas Beatie

California

© 2020 by Derek Maxfield

All rights reserved. No part of this publication may be reproduced, stored in a retrieval system, or transmitted, in any form or by any means, electronic, mechanical, photocopying, recording, or otherwise, without the prior written permission of the publisher. Printed in the United States of America.

First edition, first printing

ISBN-13 (paperback): 978-1-61121-487-1
ISBN-13 (ebook): 978-1-61121-488-8

Library of Congress Cataloging-in-Publication Data

Names: Maxfield, Derek D., author.
Title: Hellmira : The Union's Most Infamous Civil War Prison Camp–Elmira, NY / by Derek Maxfield.
Other titles: The Union's Most Infamous Civil War Prison Camp–Elmira, NY
Description: El Dorado Hills, CA : Savas Beatie, LLC, 2020. | Includes bibliographical references. | Summary: "Long called by some the "Andersonville of the North," the prisoner of war camp in Elmira, New York, is remembered as the most notorious of all Union-run POW camps. It existed for only a year-from the summer of 1864 to July 1865-but in that time, and for long after, it became darkly emblematic of man's inhumanity to man. Confederate prisoners called it "Hellmira"."-- Provided by publisher.
Identifiers: LCCN 2019051540 | ISBN 9781611214871 (paperback) | ISBN 9781611214888 (ebook)
Subjects: LCSH: Elmira Prison (Elmira, N.Y.) | Military prisons--New York (State)--Elmira--History--19th century. | New York (State)--History--Civil War, 1861-1865--Prisoners and prisons. | United States--History--Civil War, 1861-1865--Prisoners and prisons. | Prisoners of war--New York (State)--Elmira--History--19th century. | Elmira (N.Y.)--History, Military--19th century.
Classification: LCC E616.E4 M39 2020 | DDC 355.009747/78--dc23
LC record available at https://lccn.loc.gov/2019051540

Published by
Savas Beatie LLC
989 Governor Drive, Suite 102
El Dorado Hills, California 95762
Phone: 916-941-6896
Email: sales@savasbeatie.com
Web: www.savasbeatie.com

Savas Beatie titles are available at special discounts for bulk purchases in the United States by corporations, institutions, and other organizations. For more details, please contact Special Sales, 989 Governor Drive, Suite 102, El Dorado Hills, CA 95762, or you may e-mail us at sales@savasbeatie.com, or visit our website at www.savasbeatie.com for additional information.

For my parents
Duane and Vicki Maxfield
kind and generous spirits both

and

My dear grandmother
Beatrice Rogers Naylor Allen
the most loving person I have ever known

Table of Contents

Footnotes for this volume are available at
http://emergingcivilwar.com/publications/the-emerging-civil-war-series/footnotes

List of Maps

For the Emerging Civil War Series

Theodore P. Savas, *publisher*
Chris Mackowski, *series editor*
Christopher Kolakowski, *chief historian*
Sarah Keeney, *editorial consultant*
Kristopher D. White, *co-founding editor*   Design and layout by Chris Mackowski

Acknowledgments

This is my first book, and I feel a bit like the winner on one of the big award shows who feels the need to thank everyone from a kindergarten teacher to the latest acquaintance. So, I beg the reader to bear with me as I try to settle debts, professional and personal.

Beginning on the professional side, I owe the greatest debt to Chris Mackowski, editor-in-chief of the Emerging Civil War Series. I am certain that the Elmira story was originally his project, which he generously ceded to me. I am further grateful for his patience and guidance as we prepared the book for publication. My pestering, I am certain, was a burden.

Publisher Ted Savas, who has ultimate approval over books published in the series, has given much-appreciated support.

Before I go too far, I must issue a disclaimer of sorts. My object in this work focused on writing an introductory volume about Civil War prison camps in general, and the Elmira camp in particular. I have not sought to write a comprehensive study. For that, a reader must consult the books by Michael Gray, *The Business of Captivity: Elmira and its Civil War Prison* (2001), and Michael Horigan, *Elmira: Death Camp of the North* (2002). Lonnie Speer has written the definitive work on Civil War prison camps in his book *Portals to Hell: Military Prisons of the Civil War* (1997). Without these important studies, my modest volume would not have been possible.

I must thank the good folks at the Chemung Valley History Museum who aided me in my research. Education Coordinator Kelli Huggins,

Archivist Rachel Dworkin, Curator Erin Doane, and Director Bruce Whitmarsh were most welcoming and ever ready to assist. I am further indebted to Rachel Dworkin for reading the manuscript and offering valuable suggestions.

For assistance with the John W. Jones Museum and the prison site, I am indebted to John J. Corsi at the museum and Terri Olszowy and Doug Oakes at The Friends of Elmira Civil War Prison Camp. The restoration of the Jones house has been inspiring and is an important addition to Elmira's heritage. The work done at the site of the prison camp in rebuilding an original camp structure, a replica barracks, and observation platform is incredible. These visible reminders of our past go a long way toward gaining a better understanding of the Civil War. Both I and the community owe these dedicated folks a loud ovation.

Berth in the replica barracks building. Windows provided ventilation, but also an exit so men could spit tobacco. (tf)

Dr. Terrianne Schulte, Kristen and Kevin Pawlak, Michael Gosselin and Terri Olszowy contributed appendices to the project. Dr. Aaron Wheeler kindly created the maps of the camp and the overlay of the modern neighborhood. These additions enriched the book beyond measure.

I think it is necessary to say something more about my friends Terrianne Schulte and Aaron Wheeler. The former has been a friend, mentor, traveling sidekick, and intellectual sounding board for almost 20 years. Terri's patience and companionship have been a great comfort to me. Thanking her adequately seems beyond my capability. In any case, I am deeply grateful for her friendship.

Aaron Wheeler has been one of my best friends since my days in high school in the 1980s. Sadly, he lives in Florida and our get-togethers are all too infrequent. Perhaps the most intelligent person I have ever known, he nonetheless has been an important and cherished friend who is always ready to entertain my latest scheme, wine in hand.

I have had the great privilege of teaching for Genesee Community College for the past 10 years. That school, I am convinced, has the greatest collection of talent in SUNY. My colleagues on the faculty are a dedicated and hardworking lot, and they have been invariably supportive. Perhaps the greatest asset of the college though is our library staff and marketing department. In the

A mother wood duck and her ducklings take a swim on Foster's Pond. Shady and cool, the pond makes a fine place for a swim. A quiet place with little human traffic, the dense cover on the backside of the pond makes a fine home for local wildlife. (ddm)

former, I have been aided in my research by Rich Bartl, Nicki Lerczak, Cindy Francis and the good folks in the Interlibrary Loan department. The GCC "marcomm" department has always been my tireless ally and booster. Donna Rae Sutherland, the director, is my treasured friend and counselor. Her advice and support through the years has been invaluable. I am also grateful for the aid of Maureen Spindler, Tim Lawton, John Maloney, Beth Miller, and Lori Ivison.

In January 2015, it was my honor to join the stable of contributors to Emerging Civil War. More recently, I have enjoyed writing for Emerging Revolutionary War. My involvement in these enterprises reawakened a love of writing in me. To be sure, I have been inspired by the example of the talented historians who write for their blogs. I am grateful that I have been allowed entry into these exalted ranks, though on the margins.

I am often asked what inspired me to become a historian. At base, I have always been one, but there are special individuals who sparked, sustained and enlarged the interest. Although in high school my interest was primarily journalism, the social studies teachers had the most lasting influence on my life. George Tortolon, David Balch, and Nick Gigliotti in particular have my everlasting gratitude. But no one is more responsible for awakening a passion in me than the late Dr. Ellis Johnson at SUNY Cortland. "Doc" was a fantastic mentor, teacher, and friend. I have never met someone so dedicated and passionate in his calling than "Doc." Despite my inability to ever rise to his greatness, I will always measure myself against his example.

My closest friends at GCC are Tracy Ford and Michael Gosselin—both professors of English. These men have always been ready to travel to distant lands and explore vistas of my choosing. At various times, I have dragged each to Elmira to walk the ground at the prison site while I pontificate. Tracy assisted with photos and the driving tour. Moreover, the evening discussions with these good gentlemen around a fire while sipping good bourbon have sustained me through thick and thin and nourished my life of the mind. Better friends there could not be.

Finally, I owe the deepest appreciation to my family. Although they try, understanding me is no easy chore. As I live my life largely in the nineteenth century, I need to be reminded frequently that there are those in the twenty-first century that could use my attention and support. They too have trudged through cemeteries, battlefields and sites of historic import with me while I try their patience with my pedantic ramblings. My two children, daughter Quincy and son Jesse—teenagers both—are intelligent with loads of potential. It has been a pleasure to watch them grow, and I can't wait to see where life leads them.

My wife of 25 years, Christine—aka Freddie—has travelled a hard road with me over the years. I don't know how to begin to thank her. She helped sustain me through more than a dozen years of college, and now as I navigate my second decade in academia. Her patience, kindness, and love are bottomless.

PHOTO CREDITS:
Chemung County Historical Society (cchs); Find a Grave (fag); Tracy Ford (tf); *Harper's Weekly* (hw); Historical Marker Data Base/Bill Coughlin (HMDB/Bill Coughlin); Historical Marker Data Base/Scott J. Payne (HMBD/Scott J. Payne); Clay W. Holmes (ch); Historical Marker Data Base/Craig Swain (HMDB/CS); Library of Congress (loc); Chris Mackowski (cm); Derek Maxfield (ddm); Terri Olszowy (to); *Photographic History of the Civil War* (phcw); Marcus Toney, *Privations of a Private* (mt); Aaron Wheeler (aw); Wikipedia Commons (wc); Wikipedia Commons/Alan Schmierer (wc/as); Wikipedia Commons/Kolby Kirk (wc/kk)

Foreword

By Chris Mackowski

I was first introduced to the Civil War prison camp in Elmira, New York, by Stacy Keach. It was November 1982, and I was 13. Keach led an all-star cast in a three-part television miniseries called *The Blue and The Gray*, which melodramatized the Civil War for prime time consumption.

Keach played a Union intelligence officer with the square-jawed action-hero name of Jonas Steele. (Elsewhere on TV in the 80s, Keach played the similarly hard-boiled-named "Mike Hammer.") In one of the series' episodes, Jonas and his friend, John Geyser (played by John Hammond), find out that John's brother, Luke, has been transferred with other Confederate POWs to the prison camp in Elmira. During the transfer, Luke's train hit another locomotive head-on, severely injuring Luke. Survivors were bundled onto wagons and taken the rest of the way to the prison.

"They'll get no doctor in there," growls a farmerly Lloyd Bridges, who plays Luke and John's father. "From what I hear, Elmira is a Hell-hole."

Jonas, as an intelligence officer, volunteers to lead a daring ruse to free Luke from prison.

The plan, of course, goes awry, but Jonas sweeps in, all swishing cape, brass buttons, and formal orders from the War Department that may or may not be fake. He salvages the situation through charm and derring-do, and all involved make a clever getaway. The seriously injured Luke even gets to crack a joke before the segment cuts to commercial.

The Blue and The Gray's plot is crammed with

An old jokes goes like this: Why do Confederate headstones have pointed tops? Answer: To keep Yankees from sitting on them. The rows of Confederate graves at Woodlawn National Cemetery in Elmira, New York, nonetheless offer a serene setting that invites contemplation. (cm) every Civil War trope you can imagine, and the cast does justice to the stereotypes and melodrama by chewing its way through the wallpaper in every scene. Hardly a scene goes by that Keach doesn't find an excuse to cock an eyebrow or give a wry smile. Bridges brims with gravelly voice. Hammond might as well say "Gee willikers!" in every scene to underscore his over-acted naivety.

The combined effect, though, was absolutely great fun. I loved the miniseries so much I even sought out the novelization. Author John Leekley and legendary historian Bruce Catton collaborated on the original story, converted to a teleplay by Ian McLellan Hunter. On TV, Luke Geyser lay semiconscious on a cot, so grievously injured that one comrade tells another to leave Luke where he lay, where he can die among friends, rather than take him to the prison hospital where he would be murdered by enemies. "I heard the doctor bragging," the soldier gravely says. "He said he killed more Rebs than any soldier at the front."

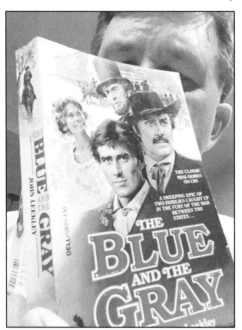

Bruce Cattton and John Leekley co-wrote the story, but Catton left the novelization to Leekley. The book has a tone closer to a magnolia-and-moonlight romance than one of Catton's award-winning historical narratives. Leekley later won an Emmy for his work as an executive producer and writer for the HBO original series *Spawn*. He's also a best-selling author and food blogger. (cm)

In the novel, Luke seems better off. Not bedridden, he hobbles around with the use of an intricately carved cane that features the date of his enlistment and a space to add the date he leaves the army. In captivity two years and four months, his spirit is so nearly broken that he contemplates touching the outer prison wall, where a signs warns, in all caps, "ANY MAN THAT TOUCHES THIS FENCE WILL BE SHOT DEAD."

"I can feel myself fading away," Luke whispers. "I can feel it."

Luke carves the day's date on the cane and prepares to return to the wall to end his captivity with a final, fateful touch. By the time Jonas and company arrive, Luke is "incredibly frail and gaunt... sick and near death." We don't know if he touched the wall or not, or how he had deteriorated so badly. There's no mention of any train wreck, though. The screenwriting team must have added it for TV.

But Jonas does still have his derring-do,

"resplendant [sic] in his new major's uniform, looking tall, polished, and very formal." He has a "gold pin" and "medals blazing against his chest," looking "as solid as if cut from granite." Again, Jonas swishes through the scene and delivers everyone to safety. He tosses the prison commandant a barb before sweeping out the door: "Captain. Do you want this cesspool of a prison investigated?"

As a cesspool, the prison looks dismal enough on TV, but the novel offers a fuller view:

> *The prison camp squatted in a low swamp of marshes and rotting trees and was surrounded by a twelve-foot-high board fence. The outside of the fence was framed by a sentry walk on which armed guards patrolled the entire perimeter.*

> *There were no trees in the camp—they had long ago been hacked down by the prisoners for firewood in their constant effort to keep warm. The ground was hard, packed down by the bare feet of thousands of men with nothing to do but walk in circles.*

> *A little stream ran through the camp, but its water barely moved in the festering mire from the latrines placed along it. A putrid smell hovered over the whole camp, and flies and mosquitoes moved in clouds above the stream.*

As prose, this was not the powerful eloquence of MacKinlay Kantor in his Pulitzer Prize-winning epic *Andersonville*, but for a mass-market paperback, it did the trick. "Hellmira," as I would later learn growing up, was often paired with its notorious Southern counterpart in discussions of Civil War prisons, as though the two made an exact comparison and somehow offering counterbalancing weight to each other on the scales of injustice.

I would also later learn that the locomotive crash in the TV version—absent from the book—was real: the Shohola train wreck.

There was much about "Hellmira" I didn't know, in fact, and for years, what I did know—or *thought* I knew—was informed by pop culture and long-repeated, perpetuated myths.

*   *   *

It didn't help that virtually nothing remained of the prison itself. During graduate school, I spent time studying the work of Mark Twain, which led me to Elmira for research at Elmira College's wonderful Center for Mark Twain Studies. Twain's wife was from Elmira, and they're both buried there. Visiting Twain's grave took me to Woodlawn Cemetery and the adjacent Woodlawn National Cemetery, where I first encountered the buried dead from the Elmira prison camp. Laid out in neat row after row, the graves made a simple, profound impression.

I returned to the cemetery frequently in subsequent years as my interest in the Civil War grew. I sought to know more about the Confederates buried in the national cemetery and the larger story of the prison camp from where they'd made their final journey.

However, the site of the former prison had vanished beneath a suburban neighborhood. Homes now stand in place of the rows of wooden bunk houses that once covered the ground. If not for a New York state historical marker in the front yard of one of those homes, along a one-way section of Water Street, a visitor could drive right by without ever knowing he was passing the prison site. A few feet away, obscured by hostas and other landscaped perennials, a granite marker installed by the Grand Army of the Republic marks the southeast corner of the prison. Several blocks north, hunkered down in a cave-like arch carved out of an evergreen hedge, another granite block marks the location of the prison's northeast corner.

"The 30-acre compound had a 12-foot stockade fence, with catwalk and sentry boxes," explains an interpretive sign that stands on ground owned by the City Water Authority one block to the west on Winsor Avenue. "There were 35 buildings, each about 100 feet long." The site had formerly been a training camp, Camp Rathbun, for New York soldiers freshly mustered into Federal service.

The Water Authority property is easy to miss, tucked along the dike that keeps the Chemung River flowing on course and out of the neighborhood. On one part of the lawn, the interpretive sign sits in a concrete shell that rises, sphere-like, from the ground. Three flagpoles, mostly obscured by trees, tower over it.

But it's the flagpole that stands a few dozen feet to the north, next to another memorial, that holds actual historical significance. It's the same flagpole that once stood inside the main gate of the prison. The original location of the flagpole is now someone's backyard (there's an ivy-covered monument there, too, not accessible to the public), but the family donated the pole itself to the city, which erected it on the Water Authority property.

The monument next to it, dedicated in May 1992, recalls the memory of "the soldiers who trained at Camp Rathbun May 1861-1864 and the Confederate Prisoners of War incarcerated at Camp Chemung July 1864-July 1865."

During the prison's 13 months of operation, more than 12,000 Confederates were incarcerated there. Some 2,900 of them died there, a death rate of 24.3%. The infamous Andersonville, by contrast, had a death toll of 29%. In Elmira, that was an average death toll of eight per day.

Two of the camp's former corners have small markers, but it's still nearly impossible to get a real sense of the size of the prison. (cm)

"Yet the striking contrast between Andersonville and Elmira should be apparent even to the most casual observer," says historian Michael Horigan, author of *Elmira: Death Camp of the North*. "Elmira, a city with excellent railroad connections, was located in a region where food, medicine, clothing, building materials, and fuel were in abundant supply. None of this could be said of Andersonville. Hence, Elmira became a symbol of death for different reasons."

Since my first attempts to track down any vestiges of "Hellmira," the Friends of Elmira Prison have reconstructed historical buildings and launched interpretive programming. The Chemung Historical Society's museum explains the camp's story and showcases artifacts that highlight that grim time. Excellent scholarship by Michael Gray, Michael Horigan, and now Derek Maxfield has peeled back the myth and misconceptions. The John Jones Museum has opened to share the

Patrick Henry Chapman came from Bedford, Virginia. He now rests far from home and family. (cm)

important story of Jones and his connections not only to the prison but the Underground Railroad.

Hellmira, slowly, has been rising from the dead.

*   *   *

My most important visit to Elmira came in 2011. A National Park Service colleague in Virginia asked if I could take a picture of an ancestor's headstone.

Patrick Henry Chapman came from Bedford, Virginia. The youngest of three brothers, they all served in Co. D of the 42nd Virginia. Chapman suffered from frostbite during the Romney campaign and remained hospitalized until just before the battle of Chancellorsville, where he was shot—along with brother John Chapman—on May 2 on the Hawkins farm during Jackson's flank attack.

Chapman returned in time for the Wilderness, although he remained with the Second Corps only long enough to get captured—again, along with John—on May 12 at Landrum Lane during the opening phase of the fight at Spotsylvania's Mule Shoe Salient.

"During the Revolution, their grandfather had been captured by the British in Charleston," my friend, Richard Chapman, told me. "I find a similarity with the Bedford Boys of D-Day and the Chapman brothers of Bedford in that brothers fought side by side in both wars and some would not return home."

Chapman first went to Point Lookout, then on August 3, was transferred to Elmira. The winter was hard on Chapman, who caught pneumonia. He died on February 27, 1865.

Using the directory at the cemetery lodge, I tracked down Chapman's grave number, 2119, and then moved among the rows of white marble headstones to find it. It looked like all the others, anonymous in its consistency until one looked closer. Like the other men here, Patrick Chapman had died far from home, buried by a former slave for $2.50.

"All war must be just the killing of strangers against whom you feel no personal animosity," Mark Twain once wrote; "strangers whom, in other circumstances, you would help if you found them in trouble, and who would help you if you needed it."

But Patrick did not feel like a stranger to me by the time I finally found him. I knew some of his story. I knew a member of his family. I knew this was not where he wanted to end up. None of them did.

Union veteran Clay MacCauley once referred to Civil War prisons as "those places of terrible memory." As terrible as memories of "Hellmira" might be, we are fortunate that recent efforts to resurrect its story renew the call to remember. It is our obligation.

The men who died here—who died at all Civil War prisons—deserve no less.

CHRIS MACKOWSKI, PH.D., *is the editor in chief of Emerging Civil War. He teaches writing at St. Bonaventure University, not too far down the road from Elmira, NY.*

Introduction

Growing up in Dundee, New York, I lived about 35 miles from the site of the POW camp in Elmira. But it was not until I was a student at SUNY Cortland, almost 10 years after graduating high school, that I discovered the fact. To me, Elmira was the home of Mark Twain and a place to go shopping—mainly at Arnot Mall.

In my ignorance, I know that I was not alone, although the Civil War was something I knew about from a fairly young age. I first discovered it when I borrowed *The Civil War*, published by National Geographic, from a great uncle. And I know it was something I learned a little about in school. But knowledge of the camp along the Chemung River eluded me. Heck, after high school I even spent a number of years working in Horseheads or Elmira, by turns, and yet did not discover anything about the camp. So far as I knew, the closest Civil War site was Gettysburg.

Of course, travelling in and around Elmira gave little indication that a prisoner of war camp that held 10,000 had ever existed—except for the National Cemetery. Even with that, there were signs for a National Cemetery here and there and that was it. You had to go into it and explore it in order to learn who it held.

In Elmira there were no historic markers for the POW camp. There were no signs pointing a visitor

Despite lacking carpentry skills of any kind, the author assists with construction of the replica barracks. (ddm)

A view of the Chemung River from the original location of the POW camp. (ddm)

to the site. And until the erection of a memorial in 1985, almost no indication that anything Civil War-related ever happened there. Even with the memorial, put up by enlightened students and citizens, you had to know it was there in order to find it.

In the late nineteenth century, stone markers were placed to mark the corners of the camp on Water Street, but again, you had to know they were there. In short, until recently, Elmira was largely scrubbed of its association with the camp and seemingly had little interest in acknowledging it. And who could blame them? How could it possibly be good for business to be known as the home of "the Andersonville of the North"?

Thankfully, from my vantage point, recent years have brought the history of the camp to light once again. Of course, the sesquicentennial of the war in 2011-15 reinvigorated an interest in the War of the Rebellion and, with it, the notion that it might not be so bad to visibly remember Barracks No. 3.

For decades, rumors had swirled that lumber from one of the Elmira prisoner of war camp buildings remained in storage and someday would be reconstructed. That this was more than rumor was confirmed in spring 2017 when I discovered the building under construction on the grounds of the Elmira Water Works on Winsor Avenue—the same property where the 1985 memorial sits. A replica of an observation tower was also under construction.

Upon investigation, I discovered that a group had been formed to raise money and finally affect the dream of digging out the original lumber and reconstructing an actual prison camp building. The Friends of the Elmira Civil War Prison Camp finished the building, using about 80% of the original lumber—some having been lost to time—and placed it on a foundation near the street. The building was dedicated June 24, 2017. But the Friends had even more ambitious plans, as it turned out.

This monument, dedicated in 1985, marks the site of the prison camp and former draft rendezvous on Winsor Avenue in Elmira. (cm)

Even before the dedication of the small prison building, plans had been hatched to construct a true-to-life replica of a prisoner barracks from dimensions and descriptions in the War Department records. And so this too has been erected on the site, less than a quarter mile from where the main gate once stood. I even had the pleasure of helping to build it (okay, one nail, but still…).

This highly-motivated band of prison camp enthusiasts now has plans to create a museum in one of the abandoned Water Works buildings near the barracks. No one is under the illusion that the site of the prison camp will become a major tourist

Replica barracks under construction at the site of the prison camp. Dimensions and characteristics of the building were discovered in War Department records. (ddm)

draw, but the efforts of this noble group will ensure that the history of the camp does not remain hidden and inaccessible.

On a personal level, I am also grateful for these efforts. I made a discovery in the past few years of a great-grandfather who served in the Civil War and was stationed in Elmira with the Veteran Reserve Corps. William B. Reese, a member of the 149th Pennsylvania "second bucktails," was wounded at Gettysburg on July 1 in the opening hours of the fight—either in the neck or the knee (the documents disagree). Never able to return to full duty, Reese was transferred to the Veteran Reserve Corps and spent his last months of the war stationed in Elmira where he stood guard over the Johnnies.

Just as I have stood on McPherson's Ridge at Gettysburg wondering just where my great-grandfather was wounded, I have more recently stood on the levy behind the Water Works staring down at Foster's Pond—taking in the now-quiet and peaceful ground. Reese was recovering from injury, but alive—one of the lucky ones. What must he have been thinking as he surveyed the human wreckage inside the camp?

While I can never know what my great-grandfather thought as he stood guard, I do know that his service in the war in general, and at the camp in Elmira, in particular, has given me a very personal connection that has shaped the way I view things and has provided the motivation to undertake this work.

A view of the reconstructed camp building, made of mostly original lumber. It is believed the building was used for housing commissary supplies. (to)

The author's third great-grandfather, William B. Reese. As a private with the 149th Pennsylvania Infantry, Reese fought and was wounded at the battle of Gettysburg before being transferred to the Veteran Reserve Corps and assigned to Elmira. (ddm)

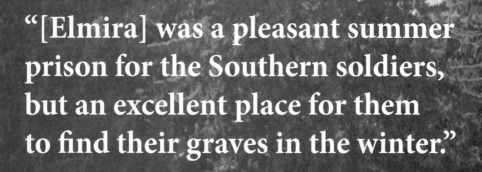

"[Elmira] was a pleasant summer prison for the Southern soldiers, but an excellent place for them to find their graves in the winter."

— *John R. King,*
Confederate Prisoner of War

Prologue

They called him "Buttons." Thomas A. Botts—a gentle, sensitive soul—arrived at Elmira as a prisoner of war in August 1864. Something of a loner, the quiet South Carolinian had sad eyes, a full beard, and lots of buttons all over his coat. The man and his buttons were a mystery to many at the compound on the Chemung.

The amiable private wandered through the camp, nonchalantly dreaming of home, but suffering from the cold wind that blew through the valley. Guards and prisoners alike could not help noticing Buttons who was "a large fine specimen of a man" wearing "a long tailed-coat of brown jeans"—covered every inch in buttons. Reluctant to explain, the quiet man tried to avoid the incessant questions. Finally, he disclosed that every button represented a Yankee he had killed.

Remembered by one prisoner as "playful as a kitten," some struggled to picture the gentle giant as a proficient killer. Yet, the coat was actually the second such garment. The first had been so filled with buttons, he had to start another.

A silent Confederate stands sentinel over the graves of Thomas Botts and more than 2,500 other southern POWs interred in Woodlawn National Cemetery. (cm)

Born in Abbeville, South Carolina in 1817, Thomas A. Botts was the son of Thomas and Nancy Botts. At the age of 31, he married Matilda Wright, and she and Botts would have five children. When war beckoned in 1861, the 44-year-old did not

Private Thomas A. "Buttons" Botts. A towering, quiet man, Botts was also a prolific killer of Yankees. (fag)

hesitate to volunteer for service with Holcombe's Legion—a South Carolina infantry regiment, Company F.

Three years after joining the Confederate bid for independence, Botts manned the trenches around Petersburg in May 1864 where he was captured. It had been a long and bloody spring for Lee's soldiers. Beginning May 5, the Overland Campaign pitted Confederate Gen. Robert E. Lee's ragged Army of Northern Virginia against the Union Army of the Potomac commanded by Maj. Gen. George Meade. The new Federal commander of all armies, Lt. Gen. Ulysses S. Grant travelled with Meade's army.

The armies clashed repeatedly over the course of the month at the Wilderness, Spotsylvania, North Anna River, and Cold Harbor before Grant ordered the Federal army to cross the James River and attempt to seize Petersburg. More or less the back door to the Confederate capital at Richmond and about 30 miles to the north, Petersburg was also an important transportation hub that was vital to the sustenance of the Confederate army.

After assaults failed to capture Petersburg, both sides settled into a siege. For many of Botts's comrades that meant long, hot days in the trenches. But the South Carolinian would not have to endure that—at least not at Petersburg. Captured at Jarrett Station on May 8, Botts soon found himself lodged at the Point Lookout prisoner of war camp in Maryland. In August, Buttons transferred to Elmira.

At Elmira in temperate August where it was probably cooler than at Petersburg, Botts likely did not suffer much from the weather at first. Boredom and dysentery were the big enemies of the prisoner. Improperly sited latrines caused polluted water and suffering for many in the Chemung pen. Chronic diarrhea and the resulting dehydration made life difficult and unpleasant for Botts and his fellow inmates.

Winter came early to the Chemung Valley, with the first snow arriving in early October 1864. Clad with a coat at least, Botts was luckier than some. An early arrival, he also likely had housing in a barracks long before others—some of whom remained in tents until January. But the bitter cold tortured a man used to the warmer clime of the Palmetto state.

Wracked with rheumatism, Botts suffered cruelly as the snow piled up. At night, with temperatures sometimes reaching ten below zero, only his coat, a blanket, and a half-inch of wood separated the slumbering giant from the outside cold. The barracks walls were not insulated or bolstered in any manner. Like all the others, Botts slept or attempted to rest on a plain pine berth with one other man. Each barracks had two stoves, but fuel to put in them was not always ample.

Inside the replica barracks built by the Friends of Elmira Prisoner of War Camp. Prisoners slept two to a bunk at each level. (tf)

The return of spring no doubt arrived as a vast relief, but all residents of the Elmira camp faced yet another challenge from Mother Nature when the Chemung River raged with spring run-off in March. With most of the camp underwater, a desperate nighttime rescue had to be endured to save those prisoners down in the smallpox hospital near the river. Botts, a big man, probably had an important hand in the operation. The jury-rigged rafts floated down to the hospital, but they had to be pulled up to the main camp by rope against a strong current. It took the help of hundreds of prisoners that night to relieve the unfortunate men who were in the wrong place at the wrong time. At least Botts got rewarded for his help with a portion of whiskey.

With the warmer weather, prisoner exchanges began again and, by May 1865, were in full swing. But the stoic Botts would not make it home. He died May 14, 1865, of unknown causes. He is buried in Woodlawn National Cemetery with more than 2,500 of his comrades beneath a bed of green, his name in marble.

The Refuse of War

CHAPTER ONE

April 1861-December 1863

The Civil War was the single greatest tragedy in American history. In four years of fighting, more than 750,000 soldiers and sailors died. During that same period over 400,000 men (and occasionally women) would be held as prisoners of war. More than 55,000 POWs died in captivity and many—though it is difficult to calculate an exact number—would perish after the war as a direct result of their mistreatment while incarcerated. In short, within the horrors of America's fraternal bloodbath lodged a humanitarian disaster of epic proportions.

At the prisoner of war camp in Elmira, New York, 2,950 prisoners died while housed along the Chemung River. The death rate of 24% made it the deadliest of the North's POW camps. In the years after the Civil War, former Confederates loudly and vociferously answered Northern obsession with the atrocities of Andersonville by calling out Elmira as the Union equivalent. Some referred to the Elmira pen as the "Andersonville of the North." Of course, Northerners stridently and self-righteously denied this charge.

However, in the last few decades historians have accepted the severity of Elmira's conditions and that much could have been done to help avert the elevated death rate. In fact, the evidence uncovered strongly suggests that a policy of retaliation existed

The Confederate Cemetery on Johnson's Island overlooks Lake Erie. Largely used to hold Confederate officers, 235 POWs perished on Johnson's Island. (loc)

A lone sentry (lower right) on patrol outside the camp. In the distance the rolling hills of the Southern Tier loom to the north. (loc)

in the Union high command (for mistreatment of Union POWs) that helps to explain why they denied Confederate POWs things like better rations. These studies are important in setting the historic record straight, showing that Elmira—and Union POW camps in general—were little better than the Confederate facilities.

Now it is time to move on from the finger pointing and the equivalent drawings. It is time to admit that Civil War prisoner of war camps, regardless of their location and who shouldered blame, practiced unnecessary inhumanity, and that both sides contributed to an enormous humanitarian disaster. Clearly, "the striking consistency of the prison experience in both the Union and Confederacy suggested that disease ravaged the prisoners and mismanagement heightened the anguish," historian Benjamin Cloyd has argued. "But the existence of these horrors resulted from deliberately cruel choices made during a war defined by callous destruction."

*   *   *

America in 1861 was entirely unprepared for large-scale war. Even as men mustered by the thousands on both sides, they made minimal preparations for dealing with mass casualties and prisoners of war. In part, this can be explained by the prevalent notion—North and South—that the war would be brief and relatively bloodless. Alabama congressman Leroy Pope Walker expressed this idea succinctly, predicting that so little blood would be spilled in a war that he could clean it up with just a pocket handkerchief.

A year into the war, and especially after the battle of Shiloh—a two-day battle at Pittsburg Landing, Tennessee that resulted in over 23,000 casualties—it was clear that a pocket handkerchief would not be adequate; perhaps all pocket handkerchiefs in America together could not cover all the bloodshed in that first year alone. There certainly were not enough doctors to attend those shedding the blood, nor were there facilities for holding prisoners.

Instrumental in the creation of the Federal prisoner of war system, Union Quartermaster General Montgomery Meigs offered valued counsel to President Lincoln. (loc)

They partly solved the first problem, lack of doctors, by recruiting men from the ranks and giving them on-the-job training. Though less than optimal, it was the best that could be done under the circumstances. However, the solution to housing prisoners of war created a complex and less easily solved situation.

As the war began, neither side had a formal policy regarding prisoners of war. Following the surrender of Fort Sumter, the Rebels paroled Major Anderson and his men—127 in all—allowing them to go north pending exchange. Even earlier, in Texas, Confederate forces had begun taking prisoners. Camp Van Dorn had been established near San Antonio to hold over 2,500 Union soldiers. Though temporary, Camp Van Dorn became the first POW camp of the Civil War. These actions, dictated by the men on the spot, did not reflect formal directives from their respective governments.

In anticipation of the battle of Bull Run fought on July 21, 1861, the Federal Quartermaster General Montgomery Meigs wrote Secretary of War Simon Cameron on July 12, suggesting the appointment of

Commander of the Union Army of the Potomac and one-time general-in-chief, Maj. Gen. George B. McClellan was a superb organizer but poor fighter. (loc)

a commissary of prisoners. "He keeps the muster-list of prisoners, negotiates exchanges according to the cartel, sends funds to the commissary of the enemy for use of our friends in their power," Meigs explained.

The question of what to do with prisoners of war pressed since Maj. Gen. George B. McClellan, commanding Union forces in western Virginia, had registered a minor victory and anticipated the need to accommodate nearly 1,000 prisoners. Writing to General-in-Chief Winfield Scott on July 13, McClellan sought instructions. "The question is an embarrassing one," McClellan wrote. "Please give me immediate instructions by telegraph as to the disposition to be made of officers and men taken prisoners of war." In response, Scott instructed McClellan to administer an oath to Confederate enlisted men, stipulating they would be paroled so long as they did not take up arms against the United States until properly exchanged. Officers would sign written paroles. However, Scott ordered that McClellan "except from this privilege all officers among your prisoners who have recently been officers of the U.S. Army or Navy and who you may have reason to believe left either with the intent of bearing arms against the United States. The captured officers of this description you will send to Fort McHenry."

Upon the recommendation of the quartermaster general, in October 1861, Lt. Col. William H. Hoffman was appointed Federal commissary general of prisoners. A distinguished officer, Hoffman had been born and raised in New York state and entered West Point as a cadet in July 1825. After graduating in 1829, Hoffman served with the 6th U.S. Infantry on frontier duty during the Black Hawk War and later in the war with Mexico. On the front lines through a number of battles—including the battles of Contreras, Churubusco, and Molino Del Rey—Hoffman earned two brevet promotions for gallant and meritorious conduct. At the outset of the Civil War, Hoffman ranked lieutenant colonel with the 8th U.S. Infantry at San Antonio, Texas. When that

regiment surrendered, Hoffman became a prisoner of war, exchanged in August 1862.

Although Jefferson Davis, president of the Confederacy, had contemplated the need to create a system for the keeping of prisoners of war, a Confederate commissary general was not appointed until 1864. Instead, Richmond Provost Marshal John H. Winder supervised prisoner of war facilities. With few exceptions, the only formal Southern facilities to accommodate prisoners early in the war stood in Richmond, mostly as converted tobacco warehouses.

Brigadier General Winder was 61 when the War of the Rebellion began. Born in Maryland, Winder had graduated from West Point and later instructed tactics there. During the Mexican War, he served as an artillery officer winning two brevet promotions for gallantry. When the War Between the States began, Winder resigned from service with the Federals to become the provost marshal of Richmond.

Lieutenant Colonel William H. Hoffman (on right), Union Commissary General of Prisoners, served as an able administrator, if a bit too frugal. (loc)

Brigadier General John H. Winder, CSA, from a pre-war photograph in a Federal uniform, had charge of the prisons in Richmond, Virginia. (loc)

In Washington, as Colonel Hoffman tried to get up to speed with his new duties, General Meigs ordered him to search for acceptable sites to establish POW camps. He would "proceed to the group of islands known as the Put-in-Bay, and Kelley's Island, off Sandusky in Lake Erie," Meigs wrote, "and to examine them with reference to the lease of the ground upon some of them for a depot for prisoners of war." Upon his return, Hoffman prepared a report on the suitability of the sites he had visited and the steps necessary to effect the creation of new camps. Interestingly, Meigs specified that the "locality selected should not be in a higher latitude than that of the west end of Lake Erie in order to avoid too rigorous a climate."

Even as Hoffman began scouting and establishing POW camps, the need to create a reliable system of exchange became apparent. In early 1862, after the fall of Forts Henry and Donelson in Tennessee, the Union faced the prospect of caring for over 15,000 prisoners. By converting old army training grounds, Hoffman moved quickly and efficiently to meet the emergency.

The battle of Shiloh, April 6-7, 1862, created difficulty for the Federal authorities when over 100,000 soldiers clashed on the Tennessee River near Pittsburg Landing.

While Shiloh was ultimately a Union victory, the costs ran high. Considered the first big battle of the war, the casualties numbered over 23,000— North and South. Union dead totaled over 1,700, with nearly 8,500 wounded and 2,885 missing or captured. Confederate losses totaled almost 10,700 with over 1,700 killed, approximately 8,000 wounded and 950 captured or missing.

The exchange of prisoners would alleviate many of the difficulties faced by both sides in housing large numbers of soldiers, but Lincoln's insistence that the Confederacy not be recognized as a sovereign power created complications. As historian Lonnie Speer pointed out, the normal "rules of conflict and the issue of what to do about prisoners did not apply" as they had during formal wars. Viewing this conflict as an insurrection also meant "captured sailors were to be considered pirates and captured soldiers would be tried for treason; both would be hanged if found guilty."

Despite these concerns, negotiations began in the summer of 1862 toward an agreement to exchange prisoners, suggesting that Lincoln recognized that his principles would be hard—if not impossible—to maintain strictly in the face of the cold, hard reality of the difficulties of holding thousands of prisoners.

John A. Dix, commissioner for the North, and D. H. Hill, commissioner for the South, reached an agreement on July 22, 1862, establishing a man-for-man exchange system with equivalencies for rank. For example, a major general would be worth 30 privates in exchange.

The exchange cartel soon operated fully, and POW camps discharged the soldiers in their care. This came as a relief to both sides, and plans to shut down various POW facilities resulted. Unfortunately, this state of affairs did not last long.

The beginning of the end for the exchange cartel came with the issuance of the preliminary Emancipation Proclamation by President Lincoln in the fall of 1862. In this important document, Lincoln changed the nature of the war dramatically by proclaiming a new goal of the war: the emancipation of slaves. By redefining the war's meaning, the president gave new hope to African-Americans, re-inspired Union men—especially Republicans, kept Great Britain from intervening in the war, and dealt a psychological blow to the Confederacy. While the proclamation had limited effect as a war order, Lincoln let it be known that if the Union won the war a constitutional amendment would seal the deal forever.

Lincoln's proclamation also opened the door to the enlistment of African-Americans in the Union army. A longtime goal of radical Republicans, former slaves and free blacks anxiously volunteered to do their part to put down the rebellion and end

This iconic print depicts the reading of the preliminary Emancipation Proclamation to Lincoln's Cabinet. The issuance of the Emancipation Proclamation on January 1, 1863, marked one of the turning points of the Civil War. (loc)

slavery forever. But the risks loomed greater than they could have anticipated, since many in the South reacted furiously to the thought of their former slaves wearing blue uniforms.

James Seddon, Confederate Secretary of War, made it clear that black soldiers could not "be recognized in any way as soldiers subject to the rules of war and to trials by military courts." Nor would many captured African-American soldiers be exchanged or paroled. In fact, the Confederacy soon began to dispose of black Union soldiers in diabolical ways—either selling them into slavery or executing them outright. In many cases, battles resulted with no black soldiers taken captive. In fact, there are accounts of black soldiers shot in the act of surrendering.

Of those who actually were taken captive, the life expectancy for a black Union soldier was grim. According to Speer, "Statistics indicate that nearly 800 black POWs were taken during the Civil War. Of those, 284—or 35%—died in captivity."

Jefferson Davis responded to Lincoln's proclamation by letting it be known that any white officers captured while leading African-American regiments in battle would "be charged with inciting a slave insurrection . . . and could even be put to death." The forcefulness of the Confederate response soon put the prisoner exchange question on shaky ground.

In May 1863, the exchange of officers ground to a complete halt after the Confederate commissioner of exchange, Robert Ould, objected to the execution of two men—Captain McGraw and Captain Corbin—convicted of spying by Union authorities. In a missive to his Union opposite, William H. Ludlow, Ould wrote and maintained that the Confederate captains had been on recruiting duty in Kentucky. As a result of the executions, Ould notified Ludlow, "The Confederate Government has ordered that two captains now in our custody shall be selected for execution in retaliation for this gross barbarity." Ould further warned that, as he understood it, Union authorities were prepared to execute others on similar charges. "In view of the awful vortex into which things are plunging," the Confederate commissioner wrote, "I give you notice that in the event of the execution of these persons retaliation to an equal extent at least will be visited upon your own officers, and if that is found ineffectual the number will be increased. The Great Ruler of nations must judge who is responsible for the initiation of this chapter of horrors."

Robert Ould, former United States Attorney for Washington, D.C., during the Buchanan administration, had attended law school at William & Mary and worked as an attorney in Washington before the war. Ould had been the prosecuting attorney in the murder trial of Dan Sickles. Sickles had shot and killed Philip Key, son of Francis Scott Key, when he discovered Key had an affair with his wife. Sickles, defended by Edwin Stanton, later U.S. Secretary of War, secured an acquittal on the plea of temporary insanity. When Virginia seceded in 1861, Ould resigned as U.S. Attorney and moved to Richmond where he became Assistant Secretary of War. In July 1862, Davis appointed Ould the chief Confederate agent of exchange.

William Ludlow, the Union agent of exchange,

Robert Ould, CSA, was the primary Confederate commissioner of exchange during the Civil War. After the war, Ould was defense attorney for Jefferson Davis when he was charged with treason, but the case never went to trial. (wc)

had been born in Yonkers, New York. He served as a New York Democratic assemblyman and had been elected Speaker of the Assembly. At the outbreak of war, Ludlow volunteered in the 73rd New York and later became an aide-de-camp to Maj. Gen. John Dix. Breveted a brigadier general, Ludlow took the position of Union agent of prisoner exchange when the cartel was established.

On May 25, 1863, Maj. Gen. Henry Halleck, the Union army's General-in-Chief, issued orders that "no Confederate officer will be paroled or exchanged until further orders." Moreover, any Confederate officers still in Union custody, though they may have already been officially exchanged, would be retained. Criminations and recriminations would be swapped by the exchange agents for some time as they each claimed that the other side had brought about this state of affairs.

Secretary of War Edwin M. Stanton, a high-powered lawyer before the war with a reputation for bold insults, mastered the art of back-stabbing. (loc)

After the summer of 1863, general exchanges of enlisted men dwindled. However, significant Union victories at Gettysburg and Vicksburg reignited the question of exchange. In the midst of these great Union triumphs, Federal Secretary of War Edwin Stanton issued an order, seeking to end paroles in the field.

Issued July 3, General Orders No. 207 recognized the general practice between opposing parties, not army commanders, to parole and release prisoners pending exchange. This was even practiced in hospitals. However, "such paroles are in violation of general orders and the stipulations of the cartel and are null and void. They are not regarded by the enemy and will not be respected in the armies of the United States. Any officer or soldier who gives such parole will be returned to duty without exchange, and moreover will be punished for disobedience of orders."

Stanton's order very likely attempted to curtail the informal, irregular use of paroles where it would be inconvenient to guard or house prisoners. Still, this use of parole was one of the problems leading to endless debate between exchange commissioners as they tried to sort it all out.

With exchanges at a standstill, the prisoners taken at Vicksburg and other environs in the west, and Gettysburg in the east presented problems. Grant had captured an entire army and paroled most of his prisoners; he only detained officers to be sent to POW camps. Shipping over 10,000 Confederate soldiers to Northern prison camps would have taken weeks and required tying up the Union navy.

In Richmond, Virginia, the Confederates converted an old tobacco warehouse near the James River into a prisoner of war facility early in the war. It became the infamous Libby Prison. (loc)

Strictly speaking, Grant accomplished the parole of the Confederate rank and file according to the cartel agreement. This meant that paroled enlisted men should have been ineligible to return to duty until formal exchange had been accomplished—a process that would take months while exchange commissioners on both sides assigned equivalents and completed the arrangement.

Waiting for the formalities to be worked out meant that thousands of desperately needed Confederate soldiers waited within the Southern states, ineligible to return to duty. Jefferson Davis found that unacceptable. "Your dispatch of yesterday received," Davis wrote to Gen. Joe

Drawing of Belle Isle, Richmond, Virginia, by artist Alfred Waud, an illustrator for *Harper's Weekly.* (loc)

Johnston. "If lists of the paroled prisoners, as heretofore directed, be promptly furnished, there will be no need to detain the men in a paroled camp, as we shall insist on immediate discharge, and give to them an opportunity again to serve their country."

Davis's unilateral decision to abandon exchange cartel protocols and simply proclaim the Confederate soldiers captured at Vicksburg exchanged sowed further seeds of distrust between Union and Confederate authorities and severely undermined prisoner exchange efforts.

Outside the unique circumstances at Vicksburg, where the capture of a whole army necessitated a parole arrangement, prisoners continued to accumulate in 1863 on both sides while the clunky exchange system sputtered. The exchange stopped and started with both sides blaming the other for the inefficiency and worsening conditions within the prison camps.

The summer of 1863 found Northern POW camps bursting at the seams and new camp construction underway. Union victories particularly challenged the established prisoner of war facilities in the Midwest. Gratiot Street in St. Louis and Illinois camps at Alton, Chicago, and Springfield all creaked under the load. Moreover, disease began to take its toll under crowded conditions.

Previously home to a medical school, Gratiot Street Prison looked much like a medieval fortress with a tower and two wings. In 1861, the provost marshal had seized the three-story stone building

due to the owner's southern sympathies and the authorities had used it as a recruiting facility before converting it to a prison.

Located near Tyler, Texas, Camp Ford held nearly 5,000 prisoners at its height; over 230 perished here. (hw)

The prison at Alton, Illinois was an abandoned penitentiary of questionable structural integrity. Dorothea Dix, who had campaigned to get the facility closed, called the place "undrained and ungraded and, generally, unsanitary." This, apparently, did not prevent its resurrection as a home for POWs.

Camp Butler in Springfield had briefly served as a POW camp in 1862, but had been shuttered. In January 1863, it reopened with a shipment of 1,600 prisoners only to swell swiftly above 2,000. Entirely without a means to warm themselves, the prisoners suffered intensely from the winter cold and had no stoves in their barracks. Before the end of March, nearly 350 died of pneumonia.

At Indianapolis, Camp Morton's official reactivation happened in 1863. Formerly a training camp for new recruits, Camp Morton transformed into a POW camp administered by the state when prisoners from Forts Henry and Donelson came in. Reopening in February 1863, Federal authorities took over the camp, intending to form a post

Gratiot Street Military Prison, located in St. Louis, Missouri, was one of the longest-serving Union facilities. More than 100 prisoners escaped from the fortress in the course of the war. (loc)

dedicated to seeing to the needs of wounded or ill POWs. Their best intentions gave way to hard reality, and soldiers of all conditions filtered in. By December 1863, Camp Morton held over 3,000 prisoners.

A somewhat similar situation occurred in Long Island Sound at David's Island. One of the Union's largest military hospitals, De Camp General Hospital kept busy in early 1863 with over 2,000 patients. After the great mid-year battles, the facility hosted Confederate wounded as well. The 80-acre site expanded as a result—stretching to fit more than 2,500 rebel prisoners.

Like Southern POW camp expansion, Union authorities added major new facilities in 1863: Point Lookout in Maryland and Rock Island on the Mississippi River in Illinois. Destined to be the largest Union POW camp, holding over 20,000 prisoners at its peak, Point Lookout was originally christened Camp Hoffman but the formal name was rarely used.

Located on an old fairground, Camp Morton in Indianapolis, Indiana, was used from 1862-65; the camp witnessed the death of more than 1,700 prisoners. (loc)

A former resort area located on a peninsula at the junction of the Potomac River and Chesapeake Bay, Point Lookout already boasted the Hammond General Hospital—one of the Union's biggest hospitals. Conveniently located and in a location relatively easy to guard, the peninsula, already leased to the Federal government, promised to be an ideal location for a prisoner of war camp.

After plotting out a 40-acre site just north of the hospital, Union officials began construction of a 15 foot high board fence to secure the camp. Two sections were created to house prisoners—one for officers and another for enlisted men. The prisoners would be sheltered in tents, though Colonel Hoffman advised the erection of wooden barracks before winter; this was never done, much to the distress of the prisoners. By December 1863, Point Lookout housed more than 9,000 Confederates.

To accommodate prisoners taken in western battles, a POW camp formed on Rock Island on the Mississippi River in late 1863. Sandwiched between Davenport, Iowa, and Moline, Illinois, the three-mile-long island was already government property. It held a U.S. arsenal and had been the home of

Historic marker for Point Lookout prisoner of war camp in Maryland. The biggest Union prisoner of war facility, the camp held nearly 22,000 Confederates at its height. (wc)

Rock Island National Cemetery, Rock Island, Illinois. First established to hold the remains of Union soldiers, the cemetery later created a Confederate section of two acres to hold the nearly 2,000 Confederate soldiers who died at the POW camp on the island. (loc)

Federal forts. Called Arsenal Island, the 950-acre land mass remained an active U.S. army facility. Prior to the Civil War, the island offered a popular picnic ground and place for a pleasant stroll. But under the press of war, and because islands were convenient places to guard, Rock Island was converted into a POW camp.

As was often the case with Union POW camps, construction of the necessary facilities at Rock Island progressed with the utmost economy. Both General Meigs and Colonel Hoffman demanded the use of rough, unfinished, and often green wood, along with other cheap materials. Quick, simple, and spartan characterized the new facilities. In total, 84 barracks were put up to hold about 120 prisoners each. Although each barracks held two coal stoves, fuel to warm them remained in perpetually short supply.

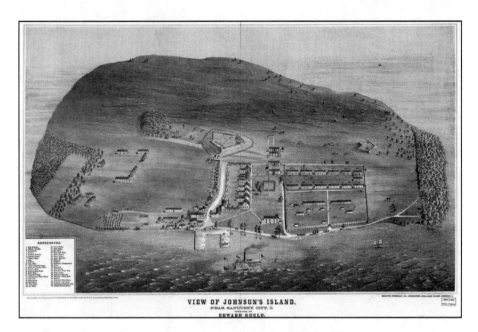

VIEW OF JOHNSON'S ISLAND,
NEAR SANDUSKY CITY, O.
EDWARD GOULD.

The lack of fuel created a real problem when the first prisoners arrived in December 1863. Almost 5,600 disembarked on the island to find two feet of snow on the ground with a temperature well below zero. The inevitable result: exposure and disease quickly took a toll.

An artist's rendering of the POW camp on Johnson's Island in Lake Erie. A steam ship can be seen bottom-center. During the summer months, it was a popular pastime to take a boat out to try to get a look at the Rebs. (loc)

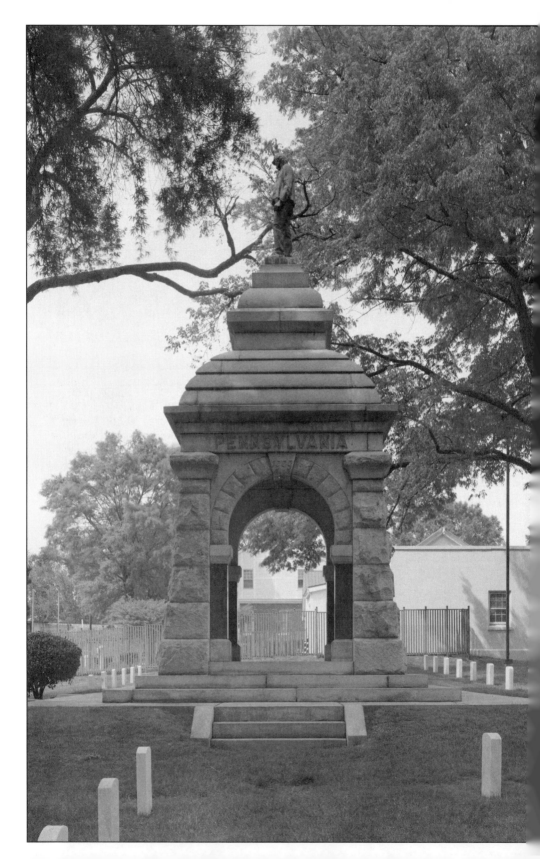

To Exchange or Not to Exchange

CHAPTER TWO

March 1864-April 1865

On March 9, 1864, Maj. Gen. Ulysses S. Grant was promoted to Lieutenant General—the third man to ever hold that rank. With the promotion came new responsibilities; now Grant replaced Halleck as General-in-Chief of all Union armies. Major General Halleck, who had held that job since 1862, became Chief of Staff. Unlike Halleck who had remained desk-bound in Washington during his tenure, Grant made his headquarters in the field near the Army of the Potomac. From that position, he coordinated simultaneous advances of Union armies in the spring campaign and directed the movements of the Army of the Potomac.

With prisoner exchange practically at a standstill, the Overland Campaign in Virginia—an almost continuous six-week battle—meant a tidal wave of new prisoners of war to be held. In this destructive campaign, the Army of the Potomac suffered over 65,000 casualties while Lee's Army of Northern Virginia lost about 35,000. On paper, Lee's losses seem significantly lighter than Grant's, but the Confederate losses totaled over 50% of the force available. With Lee unable to replace his losses, it became a matter of simple arithmetic.

As a precaution against Union raids, Confederate authorities in Richmond mined Libby Prison and threatened to blow it and everyone inside it sky-high if Union operatives tried to free POWs

The Pennsylvania monument at Salisbury National Cemetery in North Carolina. Erected in 1909, the 40-foot obelisk memorializes the 736 Pennsylvania men who died at Salisbury POW camp. (loc)

Ulysses S. Grant was one of only three men to hold the rank of lieutenant general; George Washington and Winfield Scott (by brevet) were the first two. (loc)

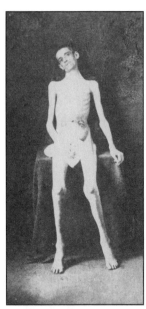

Private William M. Smith, USA, 8th Kentucky Infantry, formerly a prisoner at Belle Isle, near Richmond. (loc)

there. According to Lt. Col. Charles Farnsworth from the 1st Connecticut Cavalry and a prisoner at Libby, "We were informed one morning by negroes who labor around the prison that during the night they had been engaged in excavating a large hole under the center of the building and that a quantity of powder had been placed therein."

The POW camp at Belle Isle also sat within possible reach of Union raiders with as many as 10,000 Union soldiers languishing and wishing for escape or rescue. Conditions at this six-acre plot on the James River were miserable. Dysentery and chronic diarrhea plagued many. According to a Confederate surgeon attending the inmates, "nearly 90 percent weighed less than 100 pounds."

Belle Isle's evacuation began on February 7, 1864, and the prisoners struggled into the railroad cars for a long trip south to Andersonville, Georgia. By the end of March, Belle Isle stood vacant, and no longer a temptation for roving Union cavalry.

While Richmond's POWs were removed and populations of those prisons declined, Salisbury prison grew. Beyond reach of Union armies, this North Carolina pen was "utterly deplorable." With nearly 50% of the prisoners without shelter and disease running rampant throughout the camp, Salisbury should not have received new prisoners. But with the war raging in Virginia, new arrivals in the fall pushed the prison population above 10,000.

Since the Confederates were unable to feed that many prisoners or to provide enough fresh water, prisoners grew gaunt. Before long a typhoid epidemic claimed 75 prisoners a day; the dead bodies were stripped naked before burial to provide clothing for their living comrades.

On a visit to Salisbury in November to inspect the facility, General Winder "declared the place entirely unfit" and halted all improvements as he searched for a new site. Unfortunately, Winder's plans never worked out and conditions at Salisbury grew worse as the harsh winter of 1864-65 exposed the prisoners to more misery. Worse, prison authorities were forced to stop issuing rations for

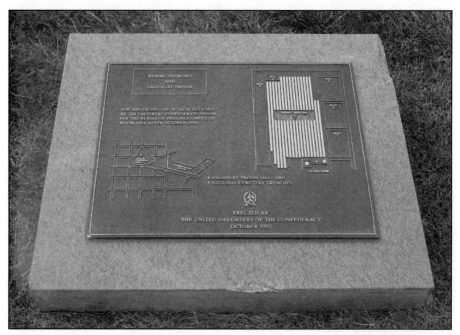

days at a time when they could not obtain more supplies.

While food availability was generally not a problem for Union officials in charge of POW camps, whether they made it available to prisoners was another matter. In fact, as a measure of retribution for Confederate mistreatment of Union POWs, the Federal war department twice reduced rations at Union-run camps. In a May 19, 1864, letter to Secretary of War Edwin Stanton, Colonel Hoffman suggested such a course:

Salisbury prisoner of war camp in North Carolina had a death rate of 25%—worse than Elmira. A modern monument offers a look at the prison's footprint and the burial trenches of its cemetery. (loc)

> *SIR: I have the honor to suggest that the ration as now issued to prisoners of war may be considerably reduced without depriving them of the food necessary to keep them in health, and I respectfully recommend that hereafter the ration be composed as follows, viz: Hard bread, 14: ounces, or 16 ounces soft bread; corn-meal, 16 ounces; beef, 14 ounces; pork or bacon, 10 ounces; beans, 6 quarts per 100 men, or rice, 8 pounds per 100 men; sugar, 12 pounds per 100 men; coffee, 5 pounds ground or 7 pounds raw per 100 men, or tea, 1 pound per 100 men; soap, 4 pounds per 100 men; salt, 2 quarts per 100 men;*

vinegar, 3 quarts per 100 men; molasses, 1 quart per 100 men; potatoes, 15 pounds per 100 men. I also recommend that ration of sugar and coffee, as above fixed, be issued only every other day.

A romanticized view of Union POWs at Salisbury, North Carolina. Built to hold 2,000, the camp bulged to more than 10,000 at one time. (loc)

In August 1864, General Winder took the unusual step of contacting Edwin Stanton directly with a proposition to relieve the suffering by prisoners on both sides. Under this plan, Federal officials would supply Confederate prisoners with all the necessary items to provide for their comfort, and the Confederate government would pay for it with cotton. In return, Federal authorities would be able to ship supplies to their soldiers in Confederate-run camps. This sly proposal offered a creative solution to the problem. Confederates, of course, did not have the supplies themselves to provide for their prisoners in Union camps due largely to the Union naval blockade. Seeing through the scheme, Maj. Gen. Ethan Allen Hitchcock, Union Commissioner of Exchange, cynically expressed surprise at the audacity of the offer. "Those authorities have systematically refused to relieve or suffer us to relieve our soldiers held as prisoners in the South," Hitchcock wrote to Stanton. "There is but one way by which relief can reach them and that is through the success of the Federal armies."

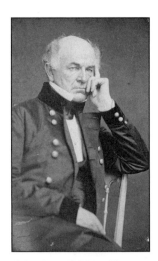

Major General Ethan Allen Hitchcock, USA, Union Commissioner of Exchange, was a renaissance man. He authored a number of books, played the flute, studied alchemy, and kept a detailed diary. (loc)

That same month Hoffman informed Stanton "that the military prisons in the East have now nearly as many prisoners in them as they can accommodate, except at Point Lookout, which can receive from 8,000 to 10,000 more." Concerned about placing more prisoners within possible reach of Confederate raiders, Hoffman proposed to build a new camp on Long Island Sound at Hart's Island, the site of a draft rendezvous.

Both sides had full prisons or facilities too

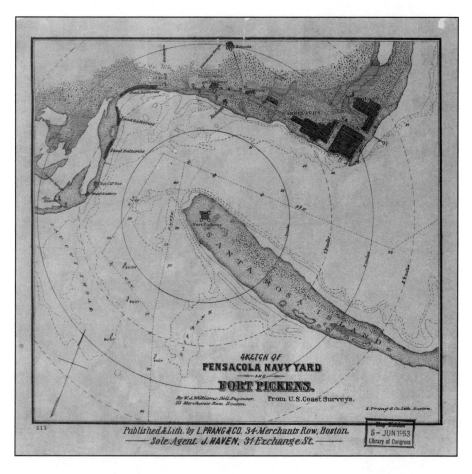

SKETCH OF
PENSACOLA NAVY YARD
—AND—
FORT PICKENS.

By W. J. Williams, Civil Engineer.   From U.S. Coast Surveys.
25 Merchants Row, Boston.

Published & Lith. by L. PRANG & CO. 34 Merchants Row, Boston.
—— Sole Agent J. HAVEN, 31 Exchange St. ——

close to the front, and they stretched out, searching for new places to house prisoners of war farther behind the lines. At the suggestion of Col. Edward Townsend, the Union Assistant Adjutant-General, the barracks at Elmira, New York, which had served as a site of a draft rendezvous, began to be considered for housing prisoners of war. With the approval of Stanton, Hoffman soon set the plan in motion.

The officers also looked beyond the snowy North for places to hold prisoners of war. Down on the Gulf of Mexico, three Federal installations— Forts Pickens, Massachusetts, and Jefferson—got slated to receive inmates.

Union Maj. Gen. Benjamin Butler's appointment as a special agent of prisoner exchange opened one of the curious chapters in the

Sketch of Fort Pickens on Santa Rosa Island, Pensacola, Florida. While the fort held prisoners of war, the population of inmates never exceeded 150. (loc)

Major General Benjamin Butler, USA, was special agent for prisoner exchange. While military governor of New Orleans, he got the nickname of "Spoons" because of his alleged habit of pocketing silverware. (loc)

history of Civil War prisoners of war. An eccentric politician from Massachusetts, Butler was an able administrator but incompetent field general. In large measure, Butler owed his position to Lincoln's need to secure support from Democrats. In 1864 with the president increasingly insecure about his reelection, he needed the support of political generals like Butler more than ever. Despite Butler's faults, Lincoln could not afford to alienate potential political allies. Unfortunately, this saddled Grant with a considerable problem.

When Butler became an agent of exchange late in 1863, he commanded the XVIII Corps at Fort Monroe. His boast that he could make things happen likely fostered his new role. The Confederate official did not welcome Butler's new position and actually took offense. The Union general had done little to endear himself and his role in the occupation of New Orleans and General Order No. 28 still lingered in Southerners' minds. "You are doubtless aware that by proclamation of the President of the Confederate States Maj. Gen. B. F. Butler is under the ban of outlawry," wrote Judge Robert Ould, Confederate Agent of Exchange, to General Hitchcock. "Although we do not pretend to prescribe what agents your Government shall employ in connection with the cartel, yet when one who has been proclaimed to be so obnoxious as General Butler is selected self-respect requires that the Confederate authorities should refuse to treat with him or establish such relations with him as properly pertain to an agent of exchange."

Butler wrote to Stanton in late December, detailing Ould's lack of cooperation. Notifying the secretary of war that he had offered the Confederate agent a generous man-for-man and rank-for-rank exchange which set aside all other disagreements—meaning the issue of the exchange of black soldiers—Butler indignantly reported that Ould would not agree to the arrangement unless the Federal government gave up its insistence on exchange equality for African-American soldiers. Further, they must "consent officially that the person to whom the Government has entrusted the command of this department shall be executed immediately upon capture, and that he and all officers serving under him shall be excluded from all the benefits of the laws which regulate civilized warfare and from even the privilege of communication by flag of truce." This, of course, Butler deemed unacceptable, and he suggested the "sternest retaliation."

For the duration of Butler's tenure, Confederate officials refused to communicate with him directly, nearly always forwarding letters to General Hitchcock or other officials. To his credit, this did not stop Butler from continuing to try to affect any exchanges possible.

In April 1864, Grant received official authority to determine policy on prisoner of war exchanges. In a message to Butler, Grant wrote, "Your report respecting negotiations with Commissioner Ould for the exchange of prisoners of war has been referred to me for my orders. Until examined by me, and my orders thereon are received by you, decline all further negotiations." Later, Grant explained his outlook:

> *It is hard on our men held in Southern prisons not to exchange them, but it is humanity to those left in the ranks to fight our battles. Every man we hold, when released on parole or otherwise, becomes an active soldier against us at once either directly or indirectly. If we commence a system of exchange which liberates all prisoners taken, we will have to fight on until the whole South is exterminated. If we hold those caught they amount to no more than dead men. At this particular time to release all rebel prisoners North would insure Sherman's defeat and would compromise our safety here.*

Aware of the intense suffering of prisoners of war on both sides, in October Judge Ould revived the scheme to use cotton to provide for Confederate prisoners of war and allowing Union authorities to send supplies to their men. This time he appealed directly to Grant, however, and received approval. While the plan had hoped to lend comfort in anticipation of the suffering that winter would bring, supplies for Confederate prisoners, purchased from the sale of cotton, did not begin to arrive until March 1865—literally too little, too late.

On the other side, much of the money and supplies sent through the lines by Union authorities for the benefit of blue-clad soldiers in Confederate prisons never got to its destination. Suspected only by May 1865, evidence appeared implicating Judge Ould, who was promptly arrested.

On February 2, 1865, Grant signaled a willingness to exchange prisoners of war again—on a large scale. Reports about the horrors at Salisbury and Andersonville undoubtedly influenced this about-face policy, but this calculated move on the general's part sowed discontent and war weariness among the people of the South in anticipation of the spring campaign.

Stereograph showing the steamer *New York* at dock, waiting for exchange of prisoners at Aiken's Landing on the James River in Virginia. (loc)

Grant knew that once the roads dried out military maneuvers would resume full force. In Virginia, this meant that Lee's much-diminished force sitting in the trenches around Petersburg would have to try to break out of the siege before it was too weak to move. When Grant had ended exchanges the year before, he worried that Southern prisoners of war would return to the ranks and bolster Confederate armies. By February 1865, this no longer concerned Grant. Very few prisoners of war on either side were fit for service after the ravages of imprisonment.

The renewal of prisoner exchanges soon made it all too clear to the general public, North and South, that both sides neglected the men in their charge. But Northern publications like *Harper's Weekly* brazenly showed the world the terrors of Andersonville and Salisbury, while at the same time arguing that Confederate POWs received good treatment. As historian Benjamin Cloyd pointed out, *Harper's Weekly* published an April 1865 "drawing of Elmira prison, in New York, complete with an American

flag waving in the breeze, [which] presented a stark contrast to the claustrophobic, graphic images that northern artists offered of the suffering individuals in the South." The drawing did not reflect the 24%

death rate at Elmira, which made some refer to it as the Andersonville of the North.

Even while the POW camps emptied, the war played out its final scenes at places like Appomattox Court House, Virginia, and Bentonville, North Carolina, where the two largest remaining Confederate armies surrendered. Abraham Lincoln's assassination overshadowed the drama of these moments, especially the surrender at Bentonville.

All told, more than 670,000 soldiers were taken captive during the War of the Rebellion. Housed in approximately 150 different locations—from local prisons to the big, open pens—at least 56,000 prisoners died during their captivity. From that conservative number, 25,796 perished in Northern facilities and another 30,218 in Southern prisons. As a percentage, it breaks down to 12% North and 15% South. The extent of loss was unnecessary, but as Cloyd argued, "Both the Lincoln and Davis administrations consistently emphasized the pragmatic needs of the war effort over humanitarian concerns for prisoner welfare. In both the Union and the Confederacy, political maneuvering and ideological expediency determined the fate of each side's captives."

A bucolic view of the Elmira POW camp in *Harper's Weekly.* **The peaceful country setting looks more like a Boy Scout camp than a prisoner of war facility.** (hw)

The Chemung Valley Plays Host

CHAPTER THREE

May 1864-August 1864

The conversion of the draft rendezvous facility in Elmira, New York, into a prisoner of war camp began shortly after Col. Edward Townsend suggested it to Hoffman in May 1864. Wasting no time, Hoffman appealed directly to the secretary of war for permission. "I respectfully suggest that one set of the barracks at Elmira may be appropriated to this purpose [of holding prisoners of war]," Hoffman wrote. "I am informed there are barracks there available which have, by crowding, received 12,000 volunteers. By fencing them in at a cost of about $2,000 they may be relied on to receive 8,000 or possibly 10,000 prisoners."

The choice of Elmira as the site of a POW camp made much sense to Union authorities at the time. The town centered at a significant railroad hub, situated well back from the front, and already had existing facilities to provide a framework to start.

Established in 1788 as the Town of Chemung, the Elmira area had been the longtime home of the Iroquois Confederacy. Pushed out during the American Revolution, most of the Native Americans in that confederacy joined forces with the British during the war, earning the ire of the new United States.

In 1808, the town was renamed "Elmira." A beneficiary of the transportation revolution, Elmira

Stairway to heaven at Woodlawn Cemetery in Elmira.
(tf)

The members of the 8th New York Militia band were among the thousands of soldiers who rendezvoused at Elmira as a muster point for the army. (cchs)

Post Commander Lt. Col. Seth Eastman, USA, was a topographical engineer and renowned artist. (loc)

became the southern terminus of the Chemung Canal which connected the Chemung River with Seneca Lake some 20 miles to the north. The New York and Erie railroad placed Elmira on a route between Buffalo and New York City in 1849. Later northern and southern spurs made the town a perfect place to serve as mustering location for new troops when the Civil War began.

In 1861, Governor Edwin Morgan designated Elmira with its bustling population nearing 9,000 as one of the three New York military depots. During July 1863, the town was named a Federal draft rendezvous. In four years, "twenty-four regiments of infantry, four companies of artillery, and six cavalry units consisting of 20,797 officers and men were mustered and trained in Elmira and transported South."

In his orders to post Commander Lt. Col. Seth Eastman, Hoffman directed that "the barracks will be enclosed by a suitable fence, and I would respectfully suggest that you construct it after the style found to be most secure at other depots. It should be eleven or twelve feet high, the frame being on the outside, with a walk for sentinels on the outside three or four feet below the top, thus giving them a good view of all that passes within."

A topographical engineer, Eastman—a native of Maine—had graduated from West Point. Assigned to Fort Snelling in Minnesota during his years after leaving the Point, Eastman took a Native American wife. In 1833, he returned to the military academy to teach drawing and meanwhile became an accomplished oil painter and illustrator. During the Mexican War, Eastman served in Texas. When the Rebels fired on Fort Sumter, the engineer got assigned recruiting duty before becoming commander of the post at Elmira.

Eastman's time in Elmira must have included some awkward moments. His second wife, Mary Henderson, was a proud descendent of the FFVs (First Families of Virginia) and from slaveholding society. She had authored the pro-slavery novel *Aunt Phillis's Cabin: or, Southern Life as it is* (1852), in response to Harriet Beecher Stowe's *Uncle Tom's Cabin*. Stowe, a frequent visitor to Elmira where her brother pastored the Park Church, would have circulated in the small elite social circles of the town with the colonel's wife.

Harriet Beecher Stowe proved to be one of the most powerful literary voices of the nineteenth century. On her frequent visits to Elmira, she circulated in the same social circles as one of her most vocal literary critics. (loc)

With some enthusiasm, Eastman prepared to house the POWs, though his directives set the new camp's capacity well below Hoffman's estimate of 8,000-10,000. "These barracks were built to comfortably accommodate 3,000 troops without crowding," Eastman wrote to Hoffman. "The bunks are double. The buildings are in excellent condition and well ventilated. Four thousand prisoners of war could be quartered in them, and there is plenty of ground room in which tents could be pitched to accommodate 1,000 more." He pointed out that a hospital would have to be provided at the barracks; Eastman further stated that the 200 men of the Veteran Reserve Corps then stationed at the barracks were entirely inadequate to guard a substantial number of POWs.

Despite his estimate of Elmira's capacity, Eastman received orders in June to prepare for 10,000 POWs. This meant substantial preparations would have to be undertaken. The former Camp Rathbun, often called Barracks No. 3 or Camp No. 3, sat on an old fairground abutting the Chemung River. Enclosing the site with a 12-foot fence that would extend 5,610 feet around the perimeter—

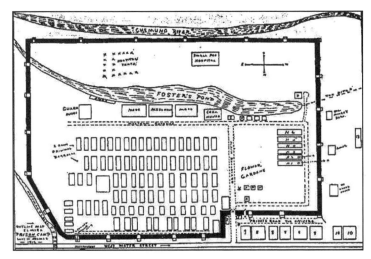

Basic outline of the Elmira POW camp on the Chemung River. The camp covered about 30 acres of ground. (loc)

including nearly 50 sentry boxes—created a major operation, but it was ready by the end of June, Eastman reported.

The first POWs arrived at Elmira on July 9, 1864, and by the middle of the month, over a thousand captives transferred from Point Lookout, Maryland. After inspecting the facility about this time, surgeon C. T. Alexander noted the problematic siting of the sinks (latrines). "They may soon become offensive and a source of disease," Alexander wrote Hoffman. "The remedy suggested is either to bring water from the city of Elmira and construct new sinks with suitable drainage, or to cause the river near which the camp is situated to communicate with the slough, thereby producing a running stream through the camp." The significance of the inspector's recommendation in his July 14 report suggested the recognition of a major health hazard. He proposed that Foster's Pond (referred to as a slough)—where the sinks were located—should be flushed and a stream of fresh water brought through the camp. This particular issue became a source of great concern as time passed, despite Alexander's suggestion in the beginning.

Alexander also noted the lack of hospital facilities and worked with Eastman to choose an appropriate site for the wards to be located. Of course, an attending surgeon would also be required. The medical cadet who currently served

A hand-drawn map of the camp from the 1860s overlays the modern neighborhood to give a sense of the size and scope of the facility. (aw)

the needs of the prisoners gave competent care, but his efforts were inadequate for the number of prisoners. Finally, the inspector suggested laying in the supplies for a 300-bed hospital.

The need for medical facilities turned out to be more pressing than anyone could have predicted. Before disease took its terrible toll, a tragic train wreck in Shohola, Pennsylvania, on July 15 resulted in the arrival of scores of wounded prisoners and guards. The train had been on the way to Elmira from Jersey City carrying over 800 prisoners from Point Lookout when it collided with a coal train. The devastating wreck killed 14 guards and 40 prisoners who had to be buried near the scene of the accident. (See account of the Shohola train wreck in Appendix C.)

Aside from the tedious tradition of marching, railroads offered the principle means of moving soldiers and supplies during the Civil War. Often rail hubs, such as Elmira, were chosen as sites for rendezvous, supply depots, and POW camps. The Erie Railroad played a vital role in the system of transporting and delivering prisoners to Elmira. Most prisoners sent to Elmira originated at Point Lookout in Maryland. First conveyed via steamer to Jersey City, they boarded the train for their journey

A modern photo of Foster's Pond. It is likely that the pond was wider in 1864 than it appears now. (tf)

to the Southern Tier. From there the cars, heavy laden with prisoners, proceeded to Port Jervis to take on fuel and water. The locomotives moved slowly through the Pocono Mountains due to the steep terrain and blind curves.

About 20 miles west of Port Jervis stood Shohola, Pennsylvania, a sleepy little town snuggled in the Poconos. On July 15, 1864, the prisoner train, running on a single rail track, was cleared to proceed at Shohola. Unfortunately, due to miscommunication, another train also ran on that track, heading east. The two trains collided head-on near King and Fuller's Cut just before 3:00 p.m.

Prisoner Anthony Keiley recalled the arrival of the survivors in Elmira. "We were roused about midnight with a request that we would come and help the wounded in, a train having arrived with the surviving victims of the catastrophe," the young Virginian wrote. "Many of them were in a horrible condition, and when I went to the hospital the following Monday I found the wounds of many still undressed, even the blood not washed from their limbs, to which, in many instances, the clothing adhered, glued by the clotted gore."

Keiley, an early arrival at Elmira, furnished the world with a first-hand account of the war and his imprisonment with fascinating insight into his experiences and treatment. A member of the Virginia House of Delegates when he was captured, Keiley had been born in New Jersey before migrating with his family to Petersburg during his boyhood. Although he had served with the Army of Northern Virginia and survived wounds from Malvern Hill, Keiley had resigned to serve in the Virginia legislature. The Yankees captured him when he turned out to assist the Petersburg militia during a Union cavalry raid. Before coming to Elmira, Keiley had spent time incarcerated at Point Lookout, Maryland.

Even before the war ended, Keiley began writing his account of his imprisonment in the North. Published just after the war, *In Vinculus; or, The Prisoner of War. Being, The Experience of a Rebel in Two Federal Pens, Interspersed With Reminiscences of the Late War; Anecdotes of Southern Generals, Etc.* is an interesting read and furnishes some invaluable, though biased, information on life at Elmira.

This guardhouse sat to the right just inside of the main prison entrance. (cchs)

View of the Elmira POW camp in the late summer of 1864 when most inmates were housed in tents. (loc)

After the conflict ended, Keiley became Mayor of Richmond and a successful attorney.

Though the Shohola victims would not be buried at Elmira until June 1911, the camp needed a plan to bury its dead. Eleven prisoners passed away before August 1, even though the camp was only weeks old, and those clearly would not be the last to die at the prison. In a letter dated July 28, Colonel Hoffman authorized the "lease [of] a half-acre lot in the Woodlawn Cemetery in Elmira, as a burying ground for deceased prisoners of war."

Eastman received authorization to spend $300 on the cemetery lease, plus more for a laborer to prepare the ground and for a proper hearse to carry the dead to Woodlawn. By January, the lease had to be expanded again by another half-acre in order to accommodate all those who expired at the camp.

Federal authorities hired John W. Jones, the sexton of Elmira cemeteries, to inter the remains of the unfortunate prisoners of the camp who died far from home. They at least received a dignified burial. Born in Loudon County, Virginia, Jones was a runaway slave who found his way to Elmira and prospered. (See a profile of Jones in Appendix B.) His prosperity would be enhanced substantially by his duties burying the dead from the camp. Instead of the $40.00 a month authorized by Hoffman,

Jones earned $2.50 for each prisoner buried at Woodlawn. In time, that totaled over $7,400.00, a tidy sum for an untidy business.

By early August, Elmira held 5,000 POWs. Reportedly in excellent condition, according to Eastman, the post had recently been reinforced by the arrival of the 54th New York militia with 350 men. Two additional New York City regiments were due anytime. The expansion of the garrison necessitated creating a new guard encampment nearby, which the commander sought permission from the War Department to do. Eastman also announced the completion of the new hospital facility.

It was an auspicious enough beginning for Elmira's new prisoner of war camp, but trouble was on the horizon for Eastman and his command. So far, the weather was warm but not unbearable, and the number of prisoners was manageable. But turmoil lay ahead for the bucolic site on the banks of the Chemung River.

John W. Jones, sexton of Woodlawn Cemetery, had the unpleasant duty to inter Confederate prisoners who died at the Elmira prison camp. The grisly task made him a rich man. (cchs)

Trouble in the Wind

CHAPTER FOUR

August 1864-December 1864

The new chief surgeon, Eugene F. Sanger, arrived just as the hospital wards were being completed, and he got right to work inspecting Barracks No. 3. Born in Waterville, Maine, in 1829, Sanger graduated from Dartmouth College and Philadelphia's Jefferson Medical School. The doctor had great ability, if not brilliance in his field, but his acerbic manner and self-satisfied personality often clashed with colleagues and superiors; his experience would be no different at Elmira.

In his inspection report of August 13, Sanger returned forcefully to the problem pointed out by surgeon Alexander a month earlier: Foster's Pond effluvia. All drainage from the camp ended up in the pond along with garbage, but the buildup of excrement was most dangerous. Observing that the construction of new sinks would alleviate some issues, Sanger still reported "seven thousand men will pass 2,600 gallons of urine daily, which is highly loaded with nitrogenous material. A portion is absorbed by the earth, still a large amount decomposes on the top of the earth or runs into the pond to purify." Disinfectant could be used to neutralize—more likely just mask—the odors, but the amount necessary would not be cost effective. "The remedy then is to pass a current of water through this putrid matter," the doctor emphasized, and warned that "unless the laws of hygiene are

A melancholy stone lady keeps watch over Woodlawn Cemetery and the hills beyond. (tf)

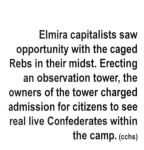

Elmira capitalists saw opportunity with the caged Rebs in their midst. Erecting an observation tower, the owners of the tower charged admission for citizens to see real live Confederates within the camp. (cchs)

carefully studied and observed in crowded camps disease is the inevitable consequence."

The laws of hygiene were not the only things studied and observed. About this time, some enterprising gentlemen erected an observation platform outside the barracks wall to allow curious locals to pay 15 cents to be able to get above the fence and view life on the inside. Many considered that a bargain price to get a look at a real Johnny Reb. Not long after, a second platform rose, and a modest rivalry ensued.

Prisoner Anthony Keiley cynically recognized the capitalist spirit in action. The platform owner "proposes to turn our pen into a menagerie, and exhibit the inmates to the refined and valorous people of the Chemung Valley," Keiley wrote in his memoir. "I am surprised Barnum has not taken the prisoners off the hands of Abe, divided them into companies, and carried them in caravans through the country."

Keiley's cynicism applied to more than just enterprising Yankees. His education and talents led his captors to entrust various jobs to him within the camp. Eventually this provided Keiley with greater status, full rations, and even good quarters on par with those of camp authorities. Even before this, the curious Virginian regularly interacted with and sought out information from the staff. On August 21, 1864, Keiley learned there had been 29 deaths the previous day and raged in his journal: "Air pure, location healthy, no epidemic," he wrote, concluding darkly, "The men are being deliberately murdered by the surgeon." Keiley added, "Especially by either the ignorance or the malice of the chief," referring to Dr. Sanger.

Keiley had a special hatred for Sanger, whom he described as "a club-footed little gentleman, with an abnormal head and a snaky look in his eyes." In the prisoner's estimation, the chief surgeon was cold and callous with an abiding dislike of rebel soldiers.

Sanger's personality grated on many people besides Keiley, but the doctor seemed to take his responsibilities seriously. He also wanted to make sure Elmira's defects would not reflect upon his reputation. Writing to Lieutenant Lounsberry, the acting assistant adjutant-general, in late August, Sanger reported almost 800 cases of scurvy out of a population of 9,300. He emphasized the necessity for "an increase of quantity and variety of antiscorbutics . . . to improve the standard of health and prevent an increase of scurvy." The doctor noted that his budget was entirely inadequate to meet the needs of the prisoners in this case. Prison authorities had to find the means to purchase the necessary vegetables. "Without change of diet we may reasonably expect an increase of scurvy," Sanger warned. "I would therefore suggest an extra issue of one ration per week of potatoes, cabbage, or onions to the prisoners for the present, and a daily issue to the scurvy cases."

Lieutenant Colonel Eastman experienced Sanger's abrasive manner and surely did not

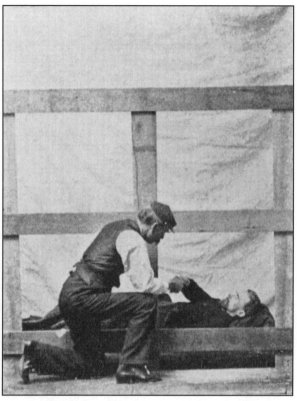

"The Dying Prisoner," as depicted in the 1907 memoir *Privations of a Private* by Marcus Toney. (mt)

Dr. Eugene F. Sanger, USA, served as chief surgeon at the Elmira prisoner of war camp. Although he had an acerbic manner, he was well respected in his field. (cchs)

appreciate his critical reports, which reflected poorly upon his management of affairs. Moreover, the post commander suffered with ill health. In fact, his health declined so rapidly that he stayed in his quarters for several weeks in early September before being relieved. He at least tried to prod Hoffman and the War Department to think ahead. "I would . . . request to be informed if any arrangement is to be made for winter quarters for prisoners of war," Eastman wrote, and also reminded them that "the troops now guarding them . . . are in tents."

Colonel Hoffman quickly pointed out to Eastman that the solution for more vegetables had already been authorized, but mostly the commissary general of prisoners believed that if the prisoners wished, they could purchase produce from the sutler to help alleviate scurvy. Hoffman, a fan of economy, offered a solution similar to his reaction to Eastman's inquiry about adding more mess halls, hospital wards, and barracks. "You are authorized to put up such hospital wards as may be indispensably necessary," Hoffman wrote, "to be built in the cheapest manner. They will not be plastered, but will be made as close as practicable by battening the joints of the weather-boarding. Barracks for the guard, or additional ones for the prisoners, will not be put up at present."

The War Department had ordered a regular system of inspections at prisoner of war camps to monitor conditions. In obedience to this, Capt. Bennett L. Munger started this duty at Elmira. In his September 25 report, Munger wrote of his concerns about the unusually cold fall along New York's Southern Tier: "The weather is cold for the season, and those in tents especially suffer. There are no stoves in quarters or hospital." Worse yet, "Those sick in quarters are fed on the ordinary prison ration, notwithstanding an order has been issued to treat them as in hospital." Clearly, Munger worried about the direction of affairs and warned, "During the past week there have been 112 deaths, reaching one day 29. There seems little doubt numbers have died both in quarters and hospital for want of proper food."

When Eastman was relieved, Col. Benjamin Tracy took over as the new post commander and responded to Munger's charge.

HEADQUARTERS DRAFT RENDEZVOUS,
Elmira, N. Y., September 30, 1864.

Respectfully forwarded to the Commissary-General of Prisoners with the following remarks: Drainage of camp is not good. There is a pond of stagnant water in the center, which renders camp unhealthy. This can be remedied by bringing water from the river through the camp. This being done, with more perfect drainage, there is no reason why the camp should not be healthy. Many men are in tents without floors or blankets. Barracks should be erected instead of tents. Hospital accommodations insufficient at present. New wards are being built. Hospital mess-rooms to accommodate about 200 patients much needed. Police of hospital good, except sinks; an offensive smell enters the tents from these. I doubt whether, with present mode of construction, this could be prevented. Scurvy prevails to a great extent. Few if any vegetables have been recently issued. Greater efforts should be made to prevent scurvy.

B. F. TRACY,
Colonel 127th U. S. Colored Troops, Commanding Depot.

Col. Benjamin F. Tracy, USA, succeeded Seth Eastman as commander of Elmira's military establishment. Previous to his posting in the Southern Tier, Tracy led the 109th New York. His heroism at the battle of the Wilderness during the Overland Campaign earned him the Congressional Medal of Honor. (loc)

Tracy's endorsement of the report is interesting for a number of reasons. First and foremost, he did not respond to the charge that men were dying of malnutrition and only commented on the prevalence of scurvy. He noted the problems caused by Foster's Pond and presented the solution of running a stream from the river—as several others had recommended since the beginning of the camp. As Eastman had already pointed out, Munger expressed concern about the housing situation of prisoners, the lack of adequate hospital facilities, and the need for more mess halls. In other words, Tracy recognized from the beginning of his tenure the very same issues that Eastman and others had complained about. It remained to be seen if the new commander would have any more luck securing the necessary facilities from authorities in Washington.

Benjamin Tracy fell into the category of those politician soldiers that Generals Grant and Sherman so disliked. A lawyer, district attorney for Tioga County, and New York state assemblyman, Tracy had been born in Owego, New York, in 1830. When the war broke out, he raised a regiment of volunteers and earned distinction in the field. During the Overland Campaign, Tracy performed heroically at the battle of the Wilderness, which later earned him the Medal of Honor. When he took command at the depot in Elmira, Tracy transferred from the position of colonel of the 127th U.S. Colored Troops.

On September 29, Tracy received from Hoffman orders stipulating that "invalid prisoners of war in your charge who will not be fit for service within sixty days will be in a few days sent South for delivery to the rebel authorities." They would prepare careful duplicate rolls and take appropriate measures for the security and well-being of the prisoners. But, Hoffman warned, "None will be sent who wish to remain and take the oath of allegiance, and none who are too feeble to endure the journey. Have a careful inspection of the prisoners made by medical officers to select those who shall be transferred."

Grant's revival of the prisoner exchange at this stage is interesting. Just months earlier, he had been vehemently opposed to the exchange because Confederate authorities refused to exchange black soldiers and from a knowledge that men on parole would be right back in the ranks of the Southern armies. This last point helps explain why only the sick, who were unable to return to service in 60 days, would be exchanged. Perhaps Grant, aware of the extent of suffering of prisoners in northern and southern camps, wanted to make a humanitarian

gesture and relieve the unfortunates wasting away. Or, with Lincoln's re-election in mind, the general-in-chief offered a political move.

Anthony Keiley, cynical as always, reacted strongly to the news of the renewal of exchange. Disappointed that he would not be among those going home, perhaps he vented his frustration as he reflected on the circumstances. "Having beat up England, Ireland, Scotland, France, Germany, Switzerland, Asia and Africa for recruits, these invincible twenty millions of Yanks admit that they still are not a match for five millions of Southerners, and they cling with the tenacity of death to every able bodied 'reb' they can clutch, lest he may again enter the Southern army." In the end, Keiley actually joined those sent south. As a parting reward from Major Colt, whom Keiley highly admired, the Virginian served as an escort and nurse for his ailing brethren on the journey.

All did not go well on the trip south for some 1,200 prisoners released from the Chemung pen. Tracy and Sanger received considerable criticism when others alleged that not enough care was taken in choosing prisoners well enough to make the grueling trip. Before arriving at Point Lookout, five prisoners died on the cars and many others lay

W. Norman, a detainee at the camp, sketched "Group of Confederate Prisoners" on September 10, 1864. (cchs)

An unknown artist depicts roll call at the camp on the Chemung. (cchs)

desperately unwell. Surgeon J. Simpson reported: "The physical condition of many of these men was distressing in the extreme, and they should never have been permitted to leave Elmira." Later, he called the negligence of Elmira officials "criminal."

As might be expected, Hoffman reacted irately about the transfer of prisoners and the fallout from it. He also felt the need to ensure that no one found him complicit in the episode. To that end, Hoffman forwarded his original instructions for Tracy to the secretary of war, which clearly showed he had specified that prisoners too sick to make the trip should not be sent south. Finally, he looked for those culpable for the tragedy. "It appears that both the commanding officer and the medical officers not only failed to be governed by these orders," Hoffman complained, "but neglected the ordinary promptings of humanity in the performance of their duties toward sick men, thus showing themselves to be wholly unfit for the positions they occupy, and it is respectfully recommended that they be immediately ordered to some other service."

Despite Hoffman's suggestion about others' incompetence and his threatening words prompted by the transfer of prisoners south, no reform action was then taken. However, over the next few months an increasingly bitter feud between Tracy and Sanger unfolded in Elmira. It seems quite possible that Tracy, and perhaps Hoffman, had marked Sanger for destruction, but waited until Sanger himself furnished more rope for the hanging.

Historian Michael Horigan, author of *Elmira: Death Camp of the North*, argued that "it was Tracy who blocked Sanger's efforts to improve hospital conditions." In a bombshell report to Brig. Gen. J. K. Barnes, Surgeon-General U.S. Army, Sanger complained at length about his situation in Elmira. "The ratio of disease and deaths has been fearfully and unprecedentedly large and requires an explanation from me to free the medical department from censure," the embittered doctor wrote. He estimated that the effective death rate since August had reached 24%, an unacceptable fact which he tried to explain through circumstances:

> *The soil is a gravel deposit sloping at two-thirds of its distance from the front toward the river to a stagnant pond of water 12 by 580 yards, between which and the river is a low sandy bottom subject to overflow when the river is high. This pond received the contents of the sinks and garbage of the camp until it became so offensive that vaults were dug on the banks of the pond for sinks and the whole left a festering mass of corruption, impregnating the entire atmosphere of the camp with its pestilential odors, night and day.*

After August 13 and shortly after Sanger arrived at Elmira, he began to submit regular reports (which he enumerated for the Surgeon-General) that reflected

Built by the Friends of the Elmira Prison Camp, the design for the replica barracks on the site came from schematics preserved in War Department records. (tf)

the problems with Foster's Pond and many other issues. Moreover, his requisitions for supplies and medicines encountered long delays or were never answered. "How does the matter stand today?" Sanger asked. "The pond remains green with putrescence, filling the air with its messengers of disease and death, the vaults give out their sickly odors, and the hospitals are crowded with victims for the grave."

One of Sanger's major complaints targeted Tracy; since that officer took command, Sanger had been unable to communicate directly with the commander. Instead, he had been told to route all communication through a "junior officer." No doubt, this inefficient system accounted for some of the delay.

As for the transfer of prisoners south and the ensuing whirlwind of recrimination, Sanger disclaimed all responsibility. He had tried to have everything in order, but had not received any information about the prisoners' trip, received no instructions, and the supplies he asked for did not get filled. Moreover, the train departed before all had been prepared. With 500 patients in the hospital, plus others out in the barracks, Sanger's days were full, and he could not be in five places at once. Sanger clearly felt that he was blocked at every turn. "I cannot be held responsible for a large medical department of over 1,000 patients without power, authority, or influence," he concluded. Something had to change. To back up his charges, Sanger had all of his assistant surgeons endorse the report.

Sanger received little satisfaction as a result of his report. Tracy ignored it, and higher authorities seemed to as well. On December 23, Sanger was relieved and probably counted himself lucky to escape such an unenviable position. "Undoubtedly," Horigan wrote, "the single greatest irony of the Elmira prison camp is this: the officer who most vociferously called attention to the unsanitary conditions and other major shortcomings of Barracks no. 3 became the nearest thing to a scapegoat in this very sad story."

Into Winter

CHAPTER FIVE

October 1864-July 1865

With a population of just over 9,000 prisoners by October 1864, only 3,800 inmates slept in barracks. All the others shivered in tents. The first snow draped the camp mid-month, pressing the need for barracks as a cold north wind chilled the bones of the poorly clad unfortunates. Thankfully, Tracy received Hoffman's permission early in the month to build additional barracks for prisoners and guards. The commissary general specified that each "building [be] 100 feet long and 22 feet broad" to accommodate 120 men with a 20 by 22 foot kitchen at the end. The new barracks would have three tiers of bunks, and the floor of each building would be elevated, so guards could see under them to prevent burrowing. As with all construction authorized by Hoffman and the War Department, the work progressed with the strictest economy. Rough wood, unfinished walls, and no insulation characterized the new barracks. To get all the prisoners under a roof, if the population did not increase dramatically, 35 additional barracks would be necessary. Although construction began immediately, the last prisoners were not in barracks until early January.

Also at the end of October, Hoffman authorized Tracy to dig a sluice connecting the river to Foster's Pond, flushing it with a stream of fresh water. Still, he continued to hope that "the

The approach of winter in Elmira, while beautiful, was very trying for the ill-clad inmates of the camp. (wc)

fall rains may be expected to come on very soon, which for this winter will do away with the necessity for the work." In a letter to Tracy, Hoffman made it clear that the authorization to fix the issue had conditions. "Make inquiries in relation to the work in all its particulars and report to me before it is commenced," Hoffman directed. "What time will it require to complete it; how many prisoners can you safely employ on it at a time; where will you obtain the necessary tools, &c.?" Astoundingly, despite the fact that Hoffman had visited Elmira and seen the scope of the problem, still he estimated that the work's cost would not exceed $120.

Tracy assured Hoffman that the work could be done quickly—only 10 to 15 days—almost entirely by prisoners with tools and materials on hand. Thus, the project began. But Tracy and Hoffman had both looked at the project idealistically. Completion of the sluice required over two months, and the cost ran over $2,000. Meanwhile, the stagnant waters continued to pollute the camp.

In an early November inspection of the camp, Colonel Munger noted that the food rations were "usually good, [although] some fresh beef has been issued unfit to eat." After Tracy's arrival, meat contracting seemed to be an issue. The inquisitive Keiley learned "that the fresh beef sent to the prison usually fell short from one thousand to twelve hundred pounds in each consignment." A lack of cattle in the Chemung valley, especially as winter approached, contributed to part of the problem, but Munger believed the beef contractor—Roger's Meat Market—dumped weak, underweight stock at the depot. A new contract somewhat rectified the situation after the current one ended at the end of the year. They defined what constituted quality beef, including the stipulation "that the cattle weigh no less than five hundred pounds." Of course, whenever the authorities rejected the beef consignment, prisoners suffered skimpier rations.

Disease, poor diet, and—with the advent of winter—exposure, took a deadly toll along the Chemung; from the camp's inception through

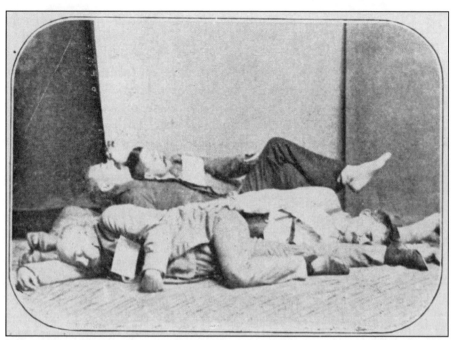

Prisoner Marcus Toney recollected his time in the smallpox ward: "The cold was below zero, and the hospital was across a little lake inside the prison walls, and the patients were in A tents—*i.e.,* tents shaped as the letter A.... I walked across the lake on the ice, and commenced my search...trying to find some bedfellows who had as light an attack as mine.... My bedfellows could not eat or drink anything, and I had all the rations, yet I could not get enough. The second night one of our bedfellows died, and all the vermin came to us, and we had plenty of company. The vermin will leave a body as soon as it gets cold. We had about eight blankets, but could not keep warm; and to make the situation worse, the men who died were dragged out and left in front of the tents, and in whatever position a man was when death overtook him in that position he froze. Some with arms and legs extended presented a horrible sight." (mt)

December 31, 1,264 prisoners perished. The inmates had the misfortune to be incarcerated during one of the harshest winters in recent memory. Snow covered the ground continually from early December through March. Despite these conditions, many prisoners lacked adequate clothing and more were without blankets, as Munger noted in his December inspection. At least by the end of the month, a clothing requisition came through. Some of the prisoners felt relief when "2,500 jackets, 2,000 pair pants, 3,011 shirts, 1,216 pair drawers, 6,065 pair socks, 3,938 blankets, 162 greatcoats" were distributed. More blankets also arrived.

As the new year arrived in Elmira, so did an unwelcome guest: smallpox. Records reported almost 100 cases with nine casualties of the disease

Maj. Henry V. Colt, USA,
was camp commandant of
Barracks No. 3 until January
1865. He returned to duty
with the 104th New York, then
part of the force besieging
Petersburg, Virginia. (cchs)

in the last week of December. Inoculation had been ongoing in the camp, but as the new Chief Surgeon Maj. Anthony Stocker noted, weak inoculant matter meant that the procedure did not always produce the intended result. Captain W. T. Hartz, Assistant Adjutant-General, authorized Tracy to erect a smallpox hospital to quarantine those suffering prisoners. Despite challenges presented by the weather, this was undertaken immediately and a small building erected for the purpose stood between Foster's Pond and the Chemung River.

A well-regarded Philadelphia physician in 1861, Stocker had been assigned to duty with the Army of the Potomac. While not nearly as abrasive as Sanger, Stocker had been twice slated for court martial, both times on slim and somewhat vague charges, suggesting that he probably had made some enemies. Sent to the Florida Keys in 1864, Stocker contracted yellow fever and went on medical leave. When he returned to duty, he journeyed to Elmira to succeed Sanger.

Although Stocker's capability went unquestioned, his tenure in Elmira stands in stark contrast to Sanger's. While Sanger was strident, insistent, and not afraid to go over the post commander's head, Stocker stayed quiet, probably a welcome change for Tracy. The camp's deficiencies did not disappear, of course. So why did Stocker seemingly accept silently what Sanger could not abide? Historian Michael Horigan wondered if a "conspiracy of silence" could have been the answer. In any case, "critics of the camp's management would at best find Stocker's lack of documentation to be suspiciously mysterious."

The new year also marked the arrival of a new camp commandant: Lt. Col. Stephen Moore. Having been reassigned, the well-respected Maj. Henry Colt departed to rejoin his comrades at the front. Colt received a parting gift from the prisoners: "An ornately designed chalice. It was whittled from a coconut shell, sat on a silver stand, and [was] engraved." Moore had actually preceded Colt in the position of camp commandant and during the latter's tenure remained at the post, commanding the guard. He was a familiar face.

William Hoffman, another familiar face, returned to the drama, though not actually at Elmira. Formerly colonel, now a brigadier general, Hoffman had been transferred to the Trans-Mississippi since November and now returned to duty in the east. On February 4, 1865, Hoffman telegrammed Tracy to prepare for prisoner transfers in groups of 3,000 by compiling name rolls at once and beginning other arrangements. For inmates at Elmira, this came as good and bad news. The prospect of going home seemed alluring, but many understood that the spring campaigns neared and that many of them would be returned to duty on the front.

Wary, Tracy still stung from the rebuke dealt him following the last transfer of prisoners south and anxiously wanted to avoid another. Replying to Hoffman, Tracy pressed for an alternate route. "The detachment of prisoners that was sent from here last fall were forty hours in reaching Baltimore, a run which should have been made in fifteen hours," the commandant explained. "To keep sick men upon the road at this season of the year in cars without seats and without water closets or any of the conveniences usually provided for the transportation of passengers will result in much suffering." Instead, Tracy advocated for shipment to New York City and from there to City Point. His suggestion fell on deaf ears.

Five hundred prisoners departed Elmira on February 13, bound for Baltimore. As before, the medical inspector found many men in desperate condition, and three had perished en route when he examined the traveling prisoners on the 15th. Tracy once again landed on the hot-seat when the finger-pointing began again. Accused a second time of neglecting his duty, Tracy pointed to the railroad company as the culprit; they had not provided light or water for those in their care. Then, he proceeded to blame the chief surgeon, who had been warned not to forward men too weak to make the journey.

Lt. Col. Stephen Moore, USA, 16th US Veteran Reserve Corps, took over the job of camp commandant in January 1865, replacing the popular Major Colt. (cchs)

Finally, he accused the weather. "It requires a pretty strong man," he argued, "to endure a railroad journey of forty-one hours during such weather as prevailed at the time this party of prisoners was forwarded." Apparently Tracy's arguments sounded credible, and the authorities said nothing more. Shipment of prisoners progressed, and by the end of March, over 3,000 inmates had been sent to Baltimore and points South.

Survival under such circumstances as prevailed at the time seemed like a roll of the dice. To stay in Elmira meant exposure to disease and weather; the death toll itself was chilling—285 died in January, 426 in February, and nearly 500 in March. Transfer to Baltimore meant braving the rigors of the trip and accommodations. Returning to the Confederacy perhaps loomed worse; most had been members of Lee's army, and the remnants of that group starved at Petersburg.

Those prisoners not transferred out of Elmira before the second week in March braved yet another hardship: water—lots of it. Warned to prepare for the rise of the river in spring, Tracy contemplated abandoning the lower camp and adjusting the compound's wall. Nothing came of that idea, probably because Hoffman refused to bear the expense. Mother Nature followed up a historic winter with a spring thaw of awesome proportions. Prisoner James Huffman in later years described the result as "the biggest flood in the history of Elmira."

The spring flood inundated the entire camp and forced prisoners in their barracks to shelter in the upper berths, staring down at four feet of brown water in some places. "All the prison walls were swept away except the side next to Elmira," Huffman recalled, "and if there had been much current some of the buildings on the hill would have gone." Tracy undoubtedly considered a full-on evacuation of the camp.

They undertook a rigorous evacuation of the smallpox hospital to rescue the poor souls stranded on what had been a spit of land next to the river.

Floating quickly-assembled makeshift rafts down from the upper camp, they rescued the endangered sick. Once loaded, the rafts were pulled back up to the main camp with ropes, fellow prisoners supplying the manpower. "The work was so strenuous," Gray wrote, "that relay teams changed every other trip and were rewarded with whiskey for their efforts."

Recalling the experience, prisoner John King remembered being "surrounded by a wilderness of water." King also reported that the men stranded in the barracks felt relieved when "after the water receded men came into our wards through the doors in row boats, passing near where we were 'roosting'. . . [and] gave us something to eat."

Finally getting rations improved the situation, but getting fresh water turned out to be a shudder-inducing occasion for King and his bunkmates. "On my way to the pump, I noticed several old blankets near my feet," King wrote. "Looking closer I discovered a number of dead men concealed under them. The high water had prevented the people from taking them to the graveyard."

The normally placid Chemung River turned into a raging torrent in March 1865, sweeping away much of the camp fencing on the river side. (loc)

Reporting to Hoffman, Tracy outlined the disaster, emphasizing that no prisoner had escaped, no building or property lost. About 2,700 feet of compound fence had been destroyed by the river and would need to be rebuilt, though this time with floodgates. The smallpox patients had been housed in old dilapidated barracks that had been abandoned. While the situation had been bad, complete disaster had been averted.

Recovery after the flood progressed slowly. Prisoners battled mud, muck, and the occasional dead fish or eel. Within weeks, the camp fence stood mended. Spring arrived, finally, and the trees of the valley again wore green. Those that survived the winter, then the flood, probably wondered at the achievement and hoped that they would not still be residents when the snowflakes began to fall again. A prisoner from the Lone Star state expressed it this way: "If ever there was a hell on earth, Elmira prison was that hell, but it was not a hot one."

The momentous events in April 1865 seemed to portend an end to prison misery. After making his escape west with the skeleton of an army, Confederate Gen. Robert E. Lee found himself surrounded at Appomattox Court House and surrendered the remainder of the Army of Northern Virginia to General Grant on April 9. The Federals also held Richmond, the Confederate capital. The war, it seemed, was ending. As prisoners at Elmira pondered these events and wondered what it meant for them, the news of Lincoln's assassination in Washington reached them.

Lincoln's death at the hands of an assassin so shortly after Lee's surrender suggested that the Confederate government might have been behind it. No one quite knew where Jefferson Davis had gone, but they knew he had fled Richmond with the Confederate treasury. In any case, the mystery and the grief of the guards and administration of the prison camp along the Chemung created a tense atmosphere. Many prisoners feared retaliation. One inmate, however, unintimidated by vengeance-minded guards declared that the assassination was "a good thing; old Abe ought to have been killed long ago!" His brash words earned him punishment: tied by his thumbs for his impudence.

On April 26, Confederate Gen. Joe Johnston surrendered his army at Bentonville, North Carolina. With the surrender of this last remaining substantial army in the South, the war moved rapidly toward its end. Meanwhile, the population still incarcerated in Elmira numbered about 5,000. The exodus from the confines of the Chemung pen proceeded slowly. In fact, though about 1,000 prisoners shipped out in May, 131 new prisoners arrived! The last of the incarcerated did not march out to board the cars headed South until July 11. On the occasion of his departure, John King recalled, "No battle-scarred veterans ever marched to victory prouder than the ragged, poorly fed, miserable 300 which passed through the big gate never to return."

Being tied up by the thumbs was, said Marcus Toney, "a very cruel mode of punishment. A man is tied up by the thumbs and pulled up till he is on his tiptoes, and there is no way to relieve the pressure. If he tries to relieve the thumbs, the toes get it; and if the toes are relieved, the thumbs are in trouble. In a very short time he will faint, and is then cut down." (mt)

A Pretty Place to Die

CHAPTER SIX

July 1864-July 1865

Not surprisingly, prison authorities and the prisoners themselves differed over the conditions at the Elmira POW camp. Looking at these sources, it must be remembered that many of the accounts about this life along the Chemung were written many years after the war. Likely, postwar events—especially the controversy over the treatment of Northern prisoners at Andersonville—influenced the memories of the former prisoners when they wrote their memoirs. With that in mind, the following two chapters focus on the prisoners' words about life in the pen and how they remembered the experience.

Upon arriving at the prison, many new inmates marveled at the natural beauty of the site. An observant man, Anthony Keiley noted that "the whole site is a basin surrounded by hills which rise several hundred feet, and are covered richly and thickly with luxurious foliage of the hemlock, ash, poplar, and pine." Prisoner James Huffman thought that "the green trees and mountains softened the landscape."

Arriving in August, prisoner Marcus Toney observed, "The prison camp contained some forty acres of land about one mile above the city, and near the Chemung River, a beautiful, clear, limpid mountain stream of very pure water." Keiley also admired the water and noted that it was "pure, cool and abundant." New prisoners "luxuriated in the

Many prisoners commented on the beauty of the Elmira area. (loc)

delicious beverage with the gusto of a lost traveler in the Sahara, or a repentant legislator after a nocturnal spree."

Of course, summer arrivals found it easy to enjoy the natural surroundings—apart from the reality of incarceration—with daytime temperatures in the seventies and eighties and pleasant overnight temperatures in the sixties and seventies. "It was a pleasant summer prison for the Southern soldiers," one prisoner admitted, "but an excellent place for them to find their graves in the winter."

Accommodations inside the pen, while not comfortable, did not present an issue at first for soldiers used to active campaigning. "We lived in low tents for the first three months, there being no houses," prisoner John King noted. But the acceptability of this arrangement quickly waned as fall arrived and temperatures began to slide. Federal authorities started putting up barracks to house prisoners, but the effort started late and construction lingered into winter.

The crudely constructed barracks at Elmira erected from rough and often green wood still gave more shelter than a tent. "The bunks were three high," Confederate Marcus Toney recalled, and "were wide-enough to sleep two medium-sized men. Each one was allowed only a pair of blankets, and so had to sleep on hard board." In especially bitter temperatures, the men often doubled up, meaning "four slept in the space of two, using one pair of blankets to sleep on, which gave three for cover."

To provide heat, two stoves sat in each barracks. Early on, these stoves uniformly burned wood, but as coal was easier to acquire, the prison administration switched over to coal stoves. On the surface, these accommodations appeared adequate, but there were flaws, as John King recalled. "The man who looked after the fires made only two fires in 24 hours." This meant that "near noon and midnight we were comfortable, but during the twelve hours between fires when the temperature of the stoves lowered, we often suffered with the cold." Still, King and his comrades counted themselves fortunate. In

their ward, the coal sergeant—a man they called "Long Tom"—treated them considerately. "Often when the weather was intensely cold and our fires were low," King remembered fondly, "our big friend would get us coal if possible."

Sometimes prisoners discovered or created unique features in the barracks. In at least one barracks, inmates "cut a little door in the side of their bunk, hinging it at the top with pieces of leather." Berry Benson, upon inquiry, found that these points were "handy to spit out of when lying in their bunks smoking, or chewing, tobacco."

The relatively late start in barracks construction added considerable suffering. Mother Nature

Before the barracks' construction, prisoners at the Elmira camp were housed in tents. Some remained in tents until January. (wc)

A prisoner wore this coat, now on display at the Chemung County Historical Society, during the frigid winter of 1864-65. (cchs)

offered no friendship to the tent-bound Southern soldier either. From prisoner accounts, summer gave way to a brief autumn and an interminably long winter. One Tar Heel soldier recorded in his diary in September that it was "very cold, worse than I have seen it in the South in the dead of winter." A Virginia soldier reported that October too brought misery. "Without even a handful of straw between them and the frozen earth," Anthony Keiley observed, "it will surprise no one that the suffering . . . was considerable."

Snow made its first appearance along the Chemung in mid-October of '64, and fell regularly at the prison until spring. "From the 1st of December to the last of February," prisoner James Huffman recorded, "all the snow that fell lay on the ground and packed down to a depth of three to four feet." If accurate, this indicated that a January thaw—fairly common in the modern era—did not occur. This seems to be sustained by the general agreement among prisoners and administrators that the winter was an unusually cold one.

Although fortunate to be housed in a barracks, John R. King, a Virginia infantryman, complained about the inadequacy of two blankets per man. "With a big snow outside and the bitter wind raging around the plank building and whistling in the cracks," winter at Elmira was an ordeal. Lack of proper footwear for the Southern-Tier Johnnies pushed matters beyond "ordeal" and amounted to torture, according to King. "In late winter, we were compelled to stand in the snow every morning for roll call," he lamented, "consequently my feet and shins were badly frozen."

A Tennessee soldier, G. W. D. Porter, recorded in his memoirs that he witnessed many of his fellow inmates suffering the effects of frostbitten hands, feet, ears, and noses. This resulted since "the mercury got down to 35 degrees below zero in the winter of 1864-65." The conditions still angered Porter over a decade after the war. Making a parallel with Native American Chief Joseph Brandt, whom he deemed a "savage," the Confederate veteran wrote

LEFT: Prisoner Marcus Toney is pictured in Union blue despite the Tennessean's Confederate allegiance. After suffering from smallpox, his Confederate duds had been burned. (mt)

that Brandt had been "tutored from his cradle to deeds of cruelty," but the Yankees boasted to being "the representatives of a civilization which [had] reached its highest type in this, the nineteenth-century of the Christian Era."

Perhaps prisoner Marcus B. Toney, another Tennessee soldier, recorded the most chilling weather. In late January 1865, Toney caught smallpox, and though he and his bunkmate tried to hide it from Union surgeons, he was discovered and exiled to the smallpox hospital. Located in what Rebel prisoners jokingly called the "Trans-Mississippi Department"—in the lowest part of the camp between Foster's Pond and the Chemung River—the smallpox ward encompassed a couple of small buildings and a few "A" tents.

"The Cold was below zero," Toney recounted, "and the hospital was across a little lake inside the prison walls . . . I walked across the lake on the ice." Placed in a bunk with two other men, both to conserve space and heat no doubt, "we had about eight blankets, but could not keep warm,"

ABOVE: Toney, as he appeared in his 1907 memoir, *Privations of a Private*, left an important chronicle of his time in Elmira. (mt)

Toney lamented. During the night one of the men died, and the Tennessean watched in horror at the handling of the body. "The men who died were dragged out and left in front of the tents," Toney recalled with a shudder, "in whatever position a man was when death overtook him in that position he froze."

While the prisoners long remembered the weather at Elmira, food got the most records with complaints about quality and quantity written at length. Every memoir included mention of it, and the accounts are uniformly damning. The only disagreement centered on who to blame. "I thought for a while that the [Union] government was retaliating on us on account of Andersonville," Toney wrote, "but I afterwards believed that it was done by the army contractors."

The normal ration, as reported by one prisoner, included: "a small piece of loaf bread and a small piece of salt pork or pickled beef each [for breakfast], and in the afternoon a small piece of bread and a tin plate of soup, with sometimes a little rice or Irish potato in the soup where the pork or beef had been broiled." At least, as Keiley wrote later, "at dinnertime, inmates were allowed to take seconds, if they chose." Not surprisingly, almost all did take advantage of it, "not that we were hungry, but merely to satisfy ourselves that the thing was real."

An even more meticulous observer recorded that he had "measured my piece of bread both in width and thickness. It was very uniform in size, exactly as thick as the distance from the end of the middle finger to the first joint inside and just as wide both ways as the length of a table knife blade, this being 5 $\frac{1}{2}$ inches wide and one $\frac{1}{2}$ inches thick." The meat ration, the same soldier reported, was "very little smaller and often we could see through the soup to the bottom of the pan." G. W. D. Porter thought what Federal authorities called soup was "in reality nothing more than hot salty water." He contended that "this salt water diet [would] account for the large number of cases of scurvy and dysentery which carried off so many."

The lean rations allotted the prisoners resulted from "reports circulated that Rebels were intentionally starving Union prisoners, and those claims seemed confirmed by the emaciated condition of many Northern prisoners after being exchanged" that spring. By the time the first prisoners arrived in Elmira, rations in all Union prison camps had been reduced by 20%. Until August, those prisoners of means had been able to supplement their rations by purchasing food from the sutler. But soon that too was restricted. Moreover, packages from home with food and/or clothing entered only for the sick.

Want of food drove men to despondency, though some more actively sought sustenance at their own hands. Throughout the camp, hunters stalked the available game—mainly rats. For those who sought the rodents, there seemed to be no shortage. The lower section of the camp, around Foster's Pond and between that and the river, offered the prime hunting ground, and men used all manner of techniques to bag their quarry.

A lively commerce in rats: one of the features of life in the Elmira pen. (mt)

Although some were disgusted by the idea of eating fresh rat, there was enough demand that they became commodities. Indeed, "many built makeshift stands from old pine boxes," according to historian Michael Gray. These hunter-capitalists "could be seen dangling a rat by the tail for prospective buyers." As unappetizing as this fare may seem, John King thought "it was well for the rat I didn't find any. They smelt very good while frying."

Occasionally, an unfortunate dog wandered into the camp, only to be devoured. For prisoner F. S. Wade, this produced a happy event because "the ribs of a stewed dog were delicious."

"The Barrel Shirt" punished by humiliation, although men driven by hunger to eat a dog might have already set their pride aside. (mt)

While the enterprising and bored might hunt and eat rat for profit and fun, it did not provide a sport for everyone. As James Huffman observed, "there were a lot of drones or life-less, do-less persons who moped about, pining away for want of sufficient food to eat, losing their humanity, eating almost anything a brute would eat . . . [even] gangrene poultices and the like." Reproducing class distinction on a smaller scale, there were those less fortunate inside the camp. J. B. Stamp, an Alabama infantryman, marveled at the phenomenon. "Apple peelings that were trampled in the mud in front of the barracks, were picked up, washed off and eaten," he remembered. "I once threw down an apple core near where some prisoners were standing and it was immediately picked up by one [prisoner] . . . and devoured."

Rebel prisoners in Elmira had a constant concern about their basic clothing. To start, the average Confederate soldier rarely boasted about being especially well-clad or shod, but incarceration worsened the situation. Prisoners arrived "thinly clad," one veteran observed, "as they came from a summer's campaign." Clearly, the Johnnies were ill-equipped for a winter in New York. "Our clothes were poor," King recalled. "The pants I had when arriving at Elmira were in such a bad condition that for a long time I wore nothing but my underwear."

In an effort to provide some measure of warmth for their charges, prison authorities

distributed old Federal overcoats, with the tails removed, to prisoners as the snow fell along the Chemung. "They helped to keep us warm," one inmate acknowledged, "but should we have been out in the world in such costume, one might have mistaken us for scarecrows eloping from the neighboring cornfield."

Undoubtedly, the inmates at the Elmira pen braved many challenges—weather, food, disease, and much more—just as Union prisoners did in Confederate prisons. Men reacted according to their natures; some found ways to get by while others gave up. Those that most successfully weathered the storm found ways to pass the time that helped to occupy their bodies and minds.

Admired by prisoners upon their arrival in the summer and fall of 1864, the beautiful surroundings turned deadly when coated in white. (loc)

Butternut Capitalists

CHAPTER SEVEN
July 1864-July 1865

Men responded to incarceration according to their natures, so long as they had their health. Without it, despondency quickly set in. "If any condition in life shows a man in his true character," one inmate wrote, "it is when he is a prisoner." According to Anthony Keiley, two outcomes, at least, could be expected. "To assemble large numbers of men in crowded quarters . . . is certain to make them hogs and very likely to make them devils."

The Elmira pen never had its "Lord of the Flies" environment to the extent of Andersonville, where prisoners preyed on each other so badly that the worst offenders were rounded up and put on trial by the prison population itself with the approbation of Commandant Wirz. Still, some of Elmira's prisoners took advantage of the weak. In particular, the theft of food, clothing, and blankets led to want and suffering.

Taking food from the mouth of a hungry man—which the prisoners called "flanking"—was strongly disapproved of by many, but persisted as a regular problem nonetheless. Others made almost a business of accumulating clothing and blankets enough for a squad, while other prisoners shivered half naked. "Many of the strongest and heartiest men would appear in the ranks almost naked," Clay Holmes reported, "which necessitated nearly

A statue of Reverend Thomas Beecher stands in front of the Park Church in Elmira, which he served for nearly 50 years. Erected in 1901, the 10-foot-tall statue was sculpted by Jonathan Scott Hartley. (tf)

Much concerned with the character of youth, Reverend Thomas Beecher formed a boy's club at the Park Church during his ministry there. Beecher was also popular with the inmates of the Elmira prisoner of war camp. (loc)

A Congregationalist minister, Reverend Henry Ward Beecher was an avid abolitionist and a popular speaker on the lecture circuit. (loc)

a complete outfit" of clothes that was then provided by the authorities. Meanwhile, back in the barracks, those same men had stashed multiple changes of clothes. Some of these same ruffians ripped blankets from men too weak to resist.

From the earliest days of the POW camp, authorities offered religious services for the butternut ragamuffins who dwelt there. The enthusiastic response of local clergymen to Eastman's suggestion that they come and preach to the multitude seemed gratifying, but not all believed their motivations were pure. Keiley observed that "the abolitionist editor in Elmira complained very bitterly of the alacrity with which the clerical gentlemen accepted the proposal, and intimated that it was due to their curiosity, not their zeal."

In general, the population of prisoners in Elmira had a religious mindset. Early on, "there are 1,511 prisoners who profess religion, 547 Baptists, 542 Methodists, 110 Presbyterians, and 242 Roman Catholics." Whatever the sect of the preacher in attendance on any occasion, the turnout was usually large and folks in the surrounding city commented on the pleasant sound occasioned by hearing thousands take up hymns.

Reverend Thomas Beecher, perhaps the most popular minister of the gospel in New York's Southern Tier, lived in the town of Elmira. Born in Litchfield, Connecticut, Beecher came from a distinguished family. Father Lyman was a respected cleric, and brother Henry Ward became one of the most famous clergymen of the nineteenth century. Beecher's sister, Harriet Beecher Stowe, authored the iconic *Uncle Tom's Cabin*. Educated in Ohio and Indiana, Thomas Beecher studied theology and chemistry before moving to Elmira in 1854 where he ministered at the Park Church.

During the war, Beecher instrumentally recruited local regiments and served in the field as chaplain of the 141st New York. Among the first to embrace the opportunity to cultivate souls inside the camp, Beecher befriended Commandant Colt and became a respected advisor. After the war Beecher became close friends with Samuel Clemens, also known as Mark Twain, and even performed the ceremony when Clemens married Olivia Langdon in 1870. (See "A Foretaste of Heaven" in Appendix E.)

While Beecher enjoyed popularity with the inmates of the pen, not all of his colleagues received the same welcome. In fact, the prisoners positively despised Reverend S. M. Bainbridge, the pastor of the Central Baptist Church. Anthony Keiley described him as "a freedom shrieker." Popular with many of the guards, Bainbridge's message devolved into "one long insult to the prisoners." When they could not abide the self-righteous sermon, many prisoners walked out. A camp officer, Lieutenant Richmond, took offense at this and arrested those that tried to leave. Although Colt overruled the arrests, Richmond's impulsive action did not endear him to the prisoners.

Although Keiley respected the Yankee clergymen that stuck close to the gospel and away from politics, he clearly disdained those like Bainbridge. "The clerical world in Puritan-dom has not changed altogether from the happy days of Quaker-whipping and Papist hanging," he complained. The abolitionist sentiment featured prominently in many Elmira preachers, including Beecher and Bainbridge, but Keiley and many of the Rebs with him were not receptive to such views.

James Huffman agreed with Keiley about the political proclivities of some Elmira clerics. "We gave good attention and enjoyed good gospels," the Virginian wrote, "but had no time to waste on old political hypocrites and would leave." Some of these ministers seemed positively "possessed with devils," Huffman believed. "Northern preachers did more to bring on the great slaughter between the states than all other forces combined."

The inmates' morals were apparently a concern, too. In addition to sending ministers into the prison, the YMCA took an active interest. According to their records, the community distributed about 4,200 New Testaments, 21,755 religious newspapers, and

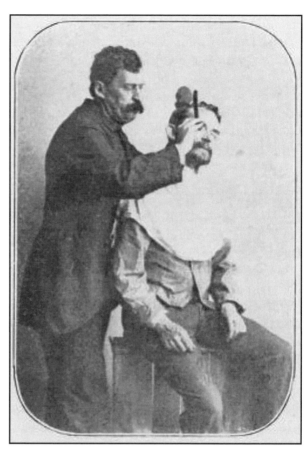

"Shave for Five Chews of Tobacco" illustrates the intricate system of barter prisoners developed for all sorts of things. (mt)

1,000 daily papers for the entertainment of the prisoners. The Rebels undoubtedly appreciated the literature. "In our circumstances," Keiley recalled, "a play-bill or a price current would have been interesting."

A lending library also emerged inside the walls of the prison. In September, the community provided a modest collection of books—probably 300 volumes. Colt and the officers in charge of the pen probably welcomed the library, seeing reading as a good alternative to tunneling. "The shelves were soon denuded of everything," Keiley wrote, "down to infantile toy-books and dilapidated geographies." Even for those who could not read, perusing the pictures undoubtedly helped to pass the time.

No reliable sources have been discovered that tell how many illiterate prisoners waited at Elmira;

accounts suggest a large number. Colonel Eastman endorsed the idea of a school inside the prison during the summer of 1864 with a prisoner who was a University of Virginia alum guiding the effort. With textbooks supplied by ladies in the community, 10 teachers among the incarcerated led the classes. While many of the classes offered elementary-level reading and writing courses, more sophisticated instruction was also available. One prisoner wrote to his wife that he enjoyed a class that taught him to speak French. Of course, if prisoners were not interested in schooling, they found any number of ways to amuse themselves and pass the time.

Still, in addition to disease, boredom stalked the residents of the camp relentlessly. "There were all kinds and mixtures of men and morals in our ward," James Huffman remembered. "Some were talking, some swearing, some singing, others playing cards, some laughing and engaged in all kinds of amusements."

The spirits and morale of these Johnnies clearly were unbroken, even though incarcerated. "We dance[d] every night at some of our quarters," prisoner Louis Leon claimed. "Some of the men put a white handkerchief around one of their arms, and these act as ladies. We had a jolly good time."

Walking through the camp, observers saw prisoners playing old standards like checkers, chess, cards, and dominoes using handmade pieces and parts. Dominoes, for example, might be made of wood or even bone. Prisoners gambled for another popular pastime, usually with cards or dice, but sometimes they staged cruder sports like lice fights or rat races.

Sometimes, projects appealed to creative prisoners. One of the earliest was a large sundial, erected in the camp near the main street that ran through the facility. Without watches, the primitive device served to let everyone know the time of day. At Point Lookout, the Union-run POW camp in Maryland, Anthony Keiley remembered one prisoner built a working locomotive using a camp kettle as a boiler. The amateur railroad engineer was

"An Ingenious Prisoner" suggests prisoners found all sorts of way to occupy themselves to alleviate boredom. (mt)

rewarded for his ingenuity when Barnum's museum purchased the train for display in New York.

In the spring of 1865, gardening was a popular pastime in Elmira. Like any city, men with a surprising array of occupations and talents called the camp their temporary home. One prisoner from Baton Rouge, Louisiana, was an expert landscape gardener. With a small army of assistants, he created sculpted lawns and intricate flower gardens just inside the main gate. This ironic beauty in such a disconsolate setting captivated many admirers.

Some prisoners whiled away the time at more profitable ventures. As prisoner L. B. Jones observed, "trinkets were made of bone, horn, gutta-percha, horse hair, and wood, into almost every conceivable thing—buttons, combs, fans, rings, watch chains, toothpicks, and many other things." The captive capitalists would engage friendly guards or prison staff to sell their wares in the town of Elmira.

Will Ellet, a local man and sympathetic agent for prison wares, drove government wagons and delivered produce and other goods into the camp. "When I began to go to the prison camp," Ellet recalled, "I had to watch my horse very closely to keep the 'Johnnies' from stealing all of the hair out of his tail." Soon, the teamster agreed to take all manner of horsehair products into town—watch-chains, rings, wreaths and more. He faithfully brought back whatever money the products sold for. Often, prisoners asked to use the profits to secure delicacies to bring back, especially pints of oysters.

They also sold their products of prison manufacture inside the camp. In fact, administrators encouraged such industry and displayed an array of goods near the main gate, where one might appreciate the skill of the inmate artisans. Also, "the market"—an area along the main street—offered a place for business transactions among the prisoners themselves.

Whether inside or outside the prison, the products created in the midst of misery were remarkable. Popular jewelry made of bone, wood, buttons, or animal hair included rings, bracelets and necklaces crafted in "the city's jewelry district." This profitable trade often did not reward those whose labor created it. Prisoners had no choice but to trust others to sell their wares; at Elmira, deceitful officers took advantage of this reality.

In his book, *The Business of Captivity: Elmira and Its Civil War Prisons*, historian Michael P. Gray wrote a riveting and insightful account of the micro economy that existed inside the walls of Elmira's prisoner of war camp. The origin of this financial system, Gray argued, stemmed from the Point Lookout experience. Because many prisoners had first been incarcerated in Maryland before coming to the Southern Tier, they brought with them a culture of enterprise. "Prisoners from Point Lookout brought such resourcefulness to Elmira: rats were

This beaded necklace was the work of a Confederate prisoner at Elmira. It is now on display at the Chemung County Historical Society and Museum. (ddm)

caught instead of crabs and tobacco regarded more highly than whiskey."

Tobacco became the currency of the Elmira pen. Divided into "chews," tobacco portions could be used to secure a haircut, clothes mended or washed, and even shoes repaired. The hungry might procure a large rat for dinner. Alcohol was not available to the New York prison and money was not allowed—though many had it.

Officially, prisoners were not to have cash. When inmates arrived at the camp, their money was taken and deposited in a system to account for it. With credits in the camp ledger, they could make purchases from the sutler from this account. When they left Elmira, prisoners received their balance in greenbacks.

Woodman Demorest—a sutler—got licensed to

operate inside the camp. In exchange for a modest commission to the camp fund, Demorest enriched himself by providing prisoners with personal necessities, food, and other goods. Over the course of the camp's existence, this sutlery earned over $50,000.

Before the War Department forbade it, Demorest offered prisoners "flour and cornmeal [which] sold at five cents a pound, cabbage at ten cents, and onions at fifteen cents a pound." He also stocked luxuries for a time. According to Gray, "one cup of milk cost fifteen cents and an apple five cents; beeswax, coffee, and sugar each sold for ten cents." The prisoners especially valued the vegetables because it allowed them to prevent scurvy—an ailment caused by a lack of vitamin C—which caused bleeding gums and ultimately the loss of teeth.

Prisoners fashioned jewelry from almost any materials they could lay hands on. The citizens of Elmira collected these crafts. (ddm)

Even when food was unavailable from the sutler, some items reliably included writing paper, stamps, pipes, and tobacco. This fortunate stock coincided with the most popular pastimes: writing letters and smoking or chewing. All letters coming in or out had to be reviewed by authorities who redacted them as necessary. Getting mail—any mail—was a godsend for prisoners and boosted their morale. Packages containing food or clothing created cause for celebration, especially as the prospect of winter in Elmira loomed, but the right to receive such packages soon ended.

Music also provided distraction and entertainment in the pen. When a German musician lamented his desire to lead a band, camp commandant Moore pulled some strings and secured donated instruments enough for 20 men. Soon, a prison band emerged, and they conducted concerts for the enjoyment of all. Later, the band traditionally played at night when retreat was sounded.

Homemade instruments were a common sight in camp, too. One inventive rebel constructed and sold fiddles made from cracker boxes and string.

Boredom: one of the prisoners' greatest enemies. To stay busy, they often created amusements from simple materials like wood or bone, like the bone die pictured here. (wc/kk)

Crude drums might be made from an old crate or a jaw harp from scrap metal.

A job in camp posed the best scenario for a prisoner, since according to Keiley, it "relieved them of the horrible ennui of imprisonment, and furnished them with the means of securing a moderate supply of tobacco." Some 400 men secured employment at Elmira at a wage of five or ten cents a day, for common labor or clerical work respectively. As an aide to Colt, Keiley ranked with the most fortunate.

Having education or skills helped ensure this work, but prisoners who swore an oath of allegiance to the United States had the greatest advantage. These galvanized Yankees also ate better, but at the cost of earning the everlasting scorn of their compatriots. Another group—Freemasons—also enjoyed preferment, especially when Moore was in command.

Despite the many possible ways of biding their time, many prisoners suffered depression, sank into despondency, and lost hope for the future, particularly during the deep, cold winter of 1864-65. A carpentry shop, opened in the center of camp, did not improve their mental state since it openly and singularly produced coffins.

Regardless of whether the rations could sustain life, the inmates waited, cut off from home, most without hope of exchange anytime soon, watching their comrades die all around them, and sitting out a war that was going decidedly against them. Even if they were exchanged, would there be a home to return to? These were sad things to contemplate. No wonder the trauma of captivity proved too much for some.

Going Home and Going Away

CHAPTER EIGHT

1865-1923

When the last prisoners departed from the camp in July 1865, about 140 were not healthy enough to travel and were confined to a hospital in Elmira. Some of them would never go home. In late September, the last prisoner, Mr. Kistler of North Carolina, started on his way home.

Colonel J. R. Lewis, 1st Veteran Reserve Corps, had to close up the camp. Tracy had resigned in early June to return to civilian life. In August, Lewis began to dispose of the components of the prison compound: the hospital wards, barracks, kitchen, and other supplies. He carried out his duties so effectively that by December no one would have known a camp had been there beside the Chemung.

Writing after the turn of the century, Clayton Holmes recalled that old camp buildings that had been acquired by citizens and turned to new uses could be recognized for many years, but by the time he wrote the history of the camp, only the old dead house could be recognized. One block away from the former camp, on West Water Street, the place prisoners studiously avoided, stood the weathered building, now with a new roof but still recognizable.

About the time Holmes composed his book, the local Grand Army of the Republic post erected—with the aid of Melvin Conklin, a former camp official—a pair of granite blocks to mark the city-side corners

After the war, the site of the prison camp was consumed by residential development. Today, a marker for the camp's east corner sits beneath a row of shrubs along West Water Street. (cm)

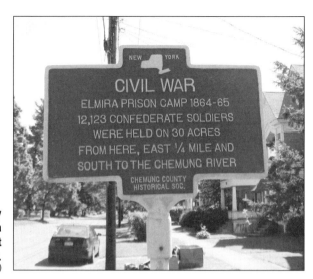

NEW YORK

CIVIL WAR
ELMIRA PRISON CAMP 1864-65
12,123 CONFEDERATE SOLDIERS
WERE HELD ON 30 ACRES
FROM HERE, EAST ¼ MILE AND
SOUTH TO THE CHEMUNG RIVER
CHEMUNG COUNTY
HISTORICAL SOC.

The Chemung County Historical Society installed a marker on West Water Street near the west corner block.
(HMDB/CS)

where the camp palisade stood. Largely hidden in the front gardens of houses on Water Street, the blocks were reminders of what once stood there.

The chief figures associated with the Elmira prisoner of war camp went on to new chapters in their lives. As is often the case with veterans of war, these men looked back on the war as a pivotal moment in their lives—for good or bad.

Brigadier General William H. Hoffman, commissary general of prisoners during the war, was brevetted a major general for his efficient service overseeing Union POW camps. Proof of this efficiency, though, revealed damning evidence against the claim that Confederate prisoners of war were well treated in Elmira. "Money withheld by Hoffman for the purchase of rations," according to Horrigan, "would result in the return of $1,845,126 to the government."[1] Hoffman returned to duty with the infantry and took command of Fort Leavenworth in Kansas. He retired in 1870 and moved to Rock Island, Illinois, where he died August 12, 1884.

Forced to retire from command of the Elmira POW camp due to ill health, Lt. Col. Seth Eastman was brevetted a brigadier general. After a moderate return to health, though he never really recovered, Eastman rejoined to paint western and Indian art for Congress and later a series of paintings depicting

prominent U.S. military forts. He died August 31, 1875, in Washington, D.C.

The last prisoners of war prepare to leave the Elmira POW camp on their way south. (ch)

In December 1864, Maj. Henry V. Colt returned to service with the 140th New York at Petersburg, Virginia, where he mustered out in January 1865. After the war, he and his family moved to Petersburg where he established a paper factory—probably with the encouragement of Anthony Keiley, former Elmira POW. When that enterprise failed, Colt returned to Elmira. For a time Colt served as deputy postmaster in Elmira. In 1872 he removed to Geneseo and went to work for the Erie Railroad where he remained until his retirement. He died in Geneseo in 1906.

Upon his retirement from command of the prison camp, Col. Benjamin Tracy was brevetted a brigadier general of volunteers. Returning to the practice of law, Tracy held the office of U.S. Attorney in New York. In 1881, the governor appointed him a judge on the New York Court of Appeals. In 1889, President Benjamin Harrison appointed Tracy Secretary of the Navy, a post he occupied for four years with considerable success; afterwards, he returned to law. Tracy died in New York City in 1915.

Initially, the men interred in the cemetery had wooden headboards to mark their graves. This photo dates circa 1875. (cchs)

After his bitter feud with Tracy, Dr. Sanger departed Elmira for new duty. Soon, he was reassigned to a military hospital in Detroit, Michigan, in Maj. Gen. Joe Hooker's department. From that post, Sanger finished his war service and then returned home to Maine. Despite his trouble getting along with superiors in the army, Sanger's medical reputation did not suffer. In fact, he went on to enjoy a distinguished medical career in Maine. He died in Bangor, Maine, on July 24, 1897.

Lieutenant Colonel Stephen T. Moore returned to his home in New Jersey after he resigned his post and took a leave. In 1866, he received orders to work with the Freedman's Bureau—a Federal agency operated by the U.S. Army to assist African-Americans with the transition to freedom. In 1869, Moore retired from the service and moved to Hammondsport, New York, where he managed a popular resort on Keuka Lake. Then, he managed another hotel in Wellsville for half a dozen years. He died in August 1891.

Some of Elmira's former inmates also enjoyed interesting and notable lives. Anthony Keiley, perhaps the most distinguished, went on to enjoy a successful law career and served as mayor of Richmond for a time. Later he would be nominated U.S. ambassador to Italy and Austria, though he never served, and would travel to Egypt where he was a justice on the International Court of Appeals. Keiley died in 1905.

Marcus B. Toney revisited Elmira in June 1913 at the invitation of Clay Holmes and regaled a large audience at the Park Church about his life inside the Chemung pen and afterwards. Settling in Nashville after the war, Toney worked in railroads for decades. An early adherent to the Ku Klux Klan, the Virginia native was also an active Mason. One of his proudest accomplishments was the founding of the Tennessee Masonic Widows' and Orphans' Home, where Toney served as its first president. Later, after his visit to Elmira, the former rebel secured passage of a bill in the U.S. Congress to place marble markers on all Confederate graves in Woodlawn Cemetery. Toney died in Nashville in 1929 at age 89.

The former camp dead house after it had been moved from the grounds of the camp and converted for private use. (cchs)

Berry Benson, who famously escaped the Elmira prison and successfully returned to duty in Virginia (see Appendix D), refused to surrender with Lee's army in April 1865. In fact, he tried to make his way to Johnston's army in North Carolina but learned of that army's surrender before reaching it. So, he took his rifle and returned home. Thereafter it was a relatively quiet life for the Georgian, who made a career as an accountant for a textile mill. Benson died near Augusta on January 1, 1923.

While the Elmira POW camp lived on in the people who worked and were incarcerated there, the physical camp disappeared from view, reclaimed as farmland and floodplain. In time, a neighborhood would grow up and the Elmira Water Works would erect buildings on the site. Few reminders of the trouble-plagued Civil War facility existed until late in the twentieth century. Across town, however, just off Davis Street, stand the unmistakable signs of war. There, emblazoned on marble headstones, are the names of the Confederate soldiers who walked in through the gates of Barracks No. 3 in 1864-65, but were carried out in pine boxes.

The Melancholy Debate
EPILOGUE

Almost 3,000 Confederate prisoners of war perished in Elmira in less than one year. The death rate of 24%—higher than any other Union POW camp—is damning and has led to many comparisons with the infamous prison pen at Andersonville where the death rate approached one-third.

Certainly, the extent of the catastrophe at Elmira appeared in the official records of the war. In particular, the medical history as researched by the Surgeon General's office, demonstrates that Barracks No. 3 not only had "a high-mortality rate, 441.1 annually per thousand of strength, but the percentage of fatal cases, 28.8, was more than double that of any other depot." Not surprisingly, dysentery and pneumonia caused the most deaths.

In the years after the war, the condition of returning POWs and grief for those that did not return occupied the hearts and minds of men on both sides. The trial, conviction, and execution of Capt. Henry Wirz, commandant of Andersonville prison, heightened the anguish and the blame game that raged for a generation. "By the end of 1865," Cloyd wrote, "Northerners viewed Andersonville and Henry Wirz as the primary symbols of Confederate atrocity. This was not coincidence— the Wirz trial represented the logical continuation of the wartime pattern in which the government manipulated the emotional controversy of Civil War prisoners for political gain."

The American flag still flies over the site of the Elmira prison camp. (cm)

Heinrich Hartmann Wirz, former commandant of Andersonville prisoner of war camp, was executed November 10, 1865, at the Old Capitol Prison in Washington, D.C. A series of photographs captured the execution. In this image, Wirz is being read his last rites. (loc)

One need not look much further for the truth in Cloyd's argument than military reconstruction of the South from 1867 to 1877. Radical Republicans in control of the U.S. Congress, who sought to punish the South for its treasonous rebellion, quickly "waved the bloody shirt" in defense of its policies. Meanwhile, carpetbaggers pillaged the South.

The more Union men harped on the atrocities at Andersonville, the more Confederates held up Elmira as the equivalent. This is well illustrated by a debate in the U.S. House of Representatives in 1876 when Congressman James G. Blaine of Maine argued that

Roll call at the Elmira POW camp. (loc)

Jefferson Davis, former president of the Confederacy, ought to be ineligible for amnesty under a bill then being considered. "Blaine wanted to exempt Davis," Gray wrote, "because he was responsible, "knowingly, deliberately, guiltily, and willfully," for the "gigantic murders and crimes at Andersonville."

In defense of Georgia, the congressman from that state, Representative Benjamin Hill, readily answered Blaine. Citing a published letter written by a Union surgeon who served at the Elmira pen, Hill spoke of the inadequate clothing of the prisoners in the midst of an "unusually severe and rigid" winter, the "turbid stream of water, carrying along with it all the excremental filth and debris of the camp," the adequate diet and resources of the area, and "yet the poor unfortunates were allowed to starve." Finally, Hill concluded, that at Elmira "a mortality

ABOVE: Congressman James G. Blaine of Maine served as one-time Speaker of the House of Representatives and later a U.S. Senator. (loc)

OPPOSITE: Woodlawn National Cemetery, circa 1933. (cchs)

equal if not greater than that of any prison in the South . . . no less . . . than Andersonville."

Like most political debates, this one produced little. Of course, both sides exaggerated and glossed over known facts. Former Elmira officials rushed into the fray, largely to defend their own reputations. The suggestion that Elmira was just as bad—in fact, the northern version of the Georgia pen—did little to acknowledge the crimes of both sides. Moreover, "[t]he consistent refusal to confront the reality of the prison atrocities," Cloyd argued, "nourished the cherished myth of American exceptionalism." The fact is that the scale of humanitarian disaster produced by American prisoner of war camps—North and South—did much to tarnish the stars on Old Glory.

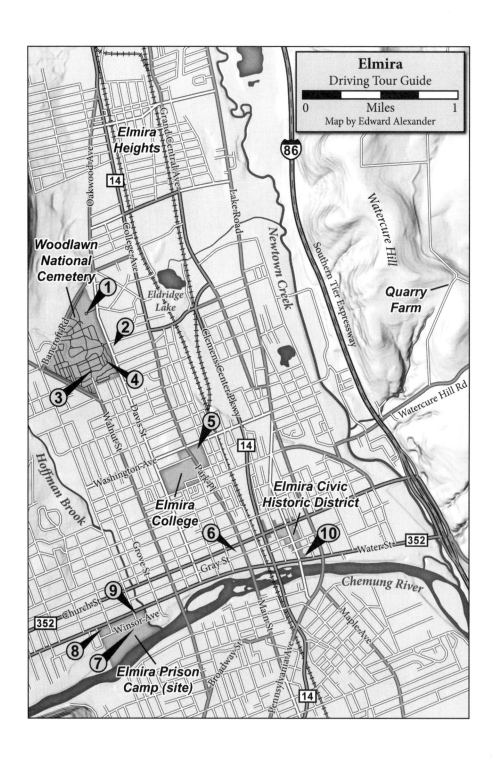

Elmira
Driving Tour Guide

0 Miles 1

Map by Edward Alexander

Elmira Heights

Woodlawn National Cemetery

Elmira Civic Historic District

Quarry Farm

Watercure Hill

Eldridge Lake

Elmira College

Elmira Prison Camp (site)

Chemung River

Hoffman Brook

Newtown Creek

Watercure Hill Rd

Southern Tier Expressway

14

86

352

352

14

Oakwood Ave

Grand Central Ave

College Ave

Lake Road

Clemens Center Pkwy

Bancroft Rd

Davis St

Walnut St

Washington Ave

Park Pl

Grove St

Church St

Winsor Ave

Broadway St

Pennsylvania Ave

Main St

Water St

Gray St

Maple Ave

Driving Tour of Elmira

APPENDIX A

The tour begins at Woodlawn National Cemetery, the most visible—and poignant—reminder of the prison camp in Elmira.

From Interstate 86 take exit 52 B to route 14 south. Turn right on 14 south and continue about 2 miles. Bear right on Oakwood Avenue (which becomes Davis Street) and continue about 1.5 miles. The cemetery will be on the right-hand side. When you turn into the gate and driveway, the prison section is off to the left.

1825 Davis Street, Elmira, NY 14901
GPS: N 42.110915, W -76.826713

Stop 1—Woodlawn National Cemetery

The portion of Woodlawn Cemetery where Confederate prisoners were buried became a national cemetery in December 1877 when the U.S. government purchased the land for $1,500. The number of burials forced the original leased half-acre to expand to two and a half acres by the

(ddm)

time the last inmate was buried. After its new designation, bodies of Union soldiers buried in other sections of Woodlawn were disinterred and moved into the national cemetery; they are buried in two rows on the north side. In time, all of the wooden grave markers were replaced with marble stones.

In 1911, the Federal government erected the Shohola monument in remembrance of those prisoners and guards killed in the tragic train wreck in Pennsylvania on July 15, 1864. Most of the victims were disinterred from their graves in Shohola and moved to Woodlawn National Cemetery in the twentieth century.

➤ TO STOP 2

Exit cemetery and turn right onto Davis Street. Continue .4 miles (one quarter mile). John W. Jones Museum will be on the left side.

1250 Davis Street, Elmira, NY 14901
GPS: N 42.10771, W -76.824524

Stop 2 – John W. Jones Museum

(ddm)

John W. Jones arrived in Elmira in July 1844 after running away from a plantation in Leesburg, Virginia where he and his family had been enslaved. After securing employment and an education, Jones became an important conductor on the Underground Railroad. As sexton of Woodlawn Cemetery, the congenial former slave had charge of burying Confederate prisoners when Elmira became home to a prisoner of war camp in 1864.

Hours vary seasonally, so please consult their website: www.johnwjonesmuseum.org.

➤ TO STOP 3

Continue south on Davis Street for .3 miles (one third of a mile) and turn right on Tompkins Street. Continue .3 miles and turn right on Walnut Street—which will lead directly into the cemetery.

Enter the cemetery on Walnut Street (drive straight in), then take the third right. Jones's grave will be on the right-hand side in section B. There are signs.

Woodlawn Cemetery, 1200 Walnut Street, Elmira, NY 14905
GPS: N 42.06340, W -76.49613

Stop 3 – Grave of John W. Jones

Jones was the sexton of Woodlawn Cemetery from its dedication in 1859 until around 1890. A dedicated conductor of the Underground Railroad, Jones may have helped as many as 800 people reach freedom. An Underground Railroad mecca, nearly every church in Elmira was involved in shuttling former slaves northward.

(ddm)

➡ **To Stop 4**

From Jones's grave, continue to T and turn right. Drive to end and turn left. The grave of Samuel Clemens (Mark Twain) and family will be on the right in section G. There are signs.

Woodlawn Cemetery, 1200 Walnut Street, Elmira, NY 14905
GPS: N 42.06376, W -76.49527

Stop 4 – Grave of Mark Twain

One of the preeminent American literary figures of the late nineteenth and early twentieth centuries, Samuel Clemens, better known as Mark Twain, authored *The Adventures of Tom Sawyer* and the *Adventures of Huckleberry Finn*. He wrote parts of these books in Elmira at Quarry

(ddm)

Farm, the home of his sister-in-law Susan Crane. In October 1870, Clemens married Olivia Langdon, daughter of abolitionist Jervis Langdon of Elmira.

Exit cemetery on Walnut Street. Continue .5 miles and turn left on W. Washington Avenue. Continue on W. Washington Avenue for .4 miles. Turn right on College Avenue (which will become Park Place). Continue on Park Place for .1 miles. Twain's study is on the left.

Twain's study sits on the campus of Elmira College. Limited parking is available along Park Place and side street.

➡ **To Stop 5**

800 Park Place, Elmira, NY 14901
GPS coordinates: N 42.05824, W -76.48840

Stop 5—Mark Twain's Study/Elmira College

(ddm)

A gift to Samuel Clemens in 1874 from Susan and Theodore Crane, his sister-in-law and brother-in-law, the octagonal study originally sat on a knoll overlooking the Chemung River on Quarry Farm. Clemens visited every summer and needed a quiet place to write and smoke his cigars. This study delighted him, and he wrote significant portions of his most famous works there. In 1952, the study was moved to the campus of Elmira College.

Hours vary; usually open daytime during the summer.

From Twain's study, travel south on Park Place for .7 miles. The church will be on the right. Parking is available on the street or on W. Gray Street.

➡ **To Stop 6**

208 W. Gray Street, Elmira, NY 14901
GPS: N 42.05368, W -76.48492

Stop 6—Park Church

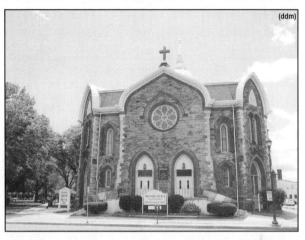

(ddm)

Opened in 1876, the Park Church is on the U.S. National Register of Historic Places and exemplifies architectural design by Horatio Nelson White. Reverend Thomas Kinnicut Beecher pastored the church until his death in 1900. Beecher served as chaplain to the 141st New York during the Civil War and later spent much time ministering to the needs of Confederate prisoners at the POW camp on the Chemung River. A bronze statue stands in his honor in Wisner Park, next to the church.

From Park Church, drive south on N. Main Street about one block (toward the Chemung River). At West Water Street, turn right and continue .6 miles. At Grove Street turn left and continue about one block. Then turn right on Winsor Avenue. Continue .2 miles and park on the street. The flagpole and monument to the camp will be on the right.

⟶ TO STOP 7

703 Winsor Avenue, Elmira, NY 14905
GPS: N 42.04948, W -76.49301 (at monument)

Stop 7—Site of the Elmira Prisoner of War Camp

Converted from a Rendezvous Camp in 1864, Barracks No. 3 was transformed for use in housing Confederate prisoners of war. For one year, July 1864 to July 1865, about 12,000 rebel soldiers called the camp "home"; nearly 3,000 died here.

Visitors will first note the red stone Municipal Water Works buildings on the south side of the street. Part of the old Winsor Pumping Station (historically noteworthy itself), these early twentieth century buildings at one time helped to provide water to Elmira Heights.

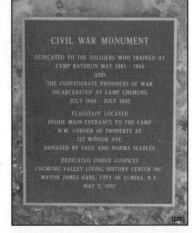

CIVIL WAR MONUMENT

DEDICATED TO THE SOLDIERS WHO TRAINED AT
CAMP RATHBUN MAY 1861 - 1864
AND
THE CONFEDERATE PRISONERS OF WAR
INCARCERATED AT CAMP CHEMUNG
JULY 1864 - JULY 1865

FLAGSTAFF LOCATED
INSIDE MAIN ENTRANCE TO THE CAMP
N.W. CORNER OF PROPERTY AT
722 WINSOR AVE.
DONATED BY PAUL AND NORMA SEARLES

DEDICATED UNDER AUSPICES
CHEMUNG VALLEY LIVING HISTORY CENTER INC
MAYOR JAMES HARE, CITY OF ELMIRA, N.Y.
MAY 3, 1992

(cm)

In 1992, this spot became a monument to the history of the Elmira POW camp. A large rock holds the dedication plaque from 1992 and, just behind it, is the original flag staff from the camp. To the right are educational panels describing the camp.

On the southern end of the property, visitors will see two buildings enclosed by a chain-link fence. There is a square building with faded yellow paint and a long rectangular building of plain wood. The former is an original camp

building that has been rebuilt by the Friends of Elmira Civil War Prison Camp. The latter is a replica of a prisoner barracks. Both buildings are occasionally opened for visitors to walk through.

Anyone interested in more information on the site of the camp or wishing to tour the buildings may consult the Friends website: www.elmiraprisoncamp. com.

⟶ TO STOP 8

Proceed west on Winsor Avenue. Turn right on Gould Street and continue to Water Street. Turn right on W. Water Street (this is a one-way, so you must turn right). The corner marker is in the yard of 811 W. Water Street, to the right of the house front amidst the foliage.

811 W. Water Street, Elmira, NY 14905
GPS: N 42.08223, W 76.82605

Stop 8–West Corner Marker

Erected by the Baldwin GAR Post #6 in 1900, this stone marker identifies the point where the northwestern corner of the camp fence stood. From this point, the fence ran all the way to the Chemung River to the south and down along W. Water Street to the point marked by the East Corner Marker.

(cm)

⟶ To Stop 9

Proceed east along W. Water Street for about two blocks. The East Corner Marker will be on the right in the yard of the first house past Hoffman Street.

641 W. Water Street, Elmira, NY 14905
GPS: N 42.08362, W 76.82156

Stop 9–East Corner Marker

Also erected by the Baldwin GAR Post #6 in 1900, this stone marker identifies the point where the northeastern corner of the camp fence stood. But while the opposite corner ran straight down to the river, the fence on this side jogged 45 degrees along a small creek—now called Hoffman Brook—before meeting another angle where the fence then proceeded south to the river.

(cm)

All told, the fence contained approximately 30 acres of ground.

⟶ TO STOP 10

Proceed east along W. Water Street approximately one mile. The Chemung Valley History Museum will be on the left.

415 E. Water Street, Elmira, NY 14901
GPS: N 42.088775, W -76.800509

Stop 10 – Chemung Valley History Museum

The largest history museum in the Chemung Valley, the Chemung Valley History Museum was founded in 1923 with a mission to preserve and perpetuate the history of the region.

The Chemung County Historical Society operates both the Chemung Valley History Museum and the Booth Library. Among the many interesting items in the collection are artifacts from the Elmira POW camp, including items made by the Confederate prisoners. Website: www.chemungvalleymuseum.org.

Hours: Monday - Saturday 10 a.m. to 5 p.m.; Closed Sundays

This concludes the tour.

To return to Interstate 86, continue east on E. Water Street about one mile. Signs will indicate onramps for east and west.

The John W. Jones
The Great Care-Taker

APPENDIX B
BY DEREK MAXFIELD

As an enslaved boy in Virginia, John W. Jones dreamed of a different world outside the plantation. "One day while the boy sat listening to the stories of his grandmother," Clay Holmes wrote, "a flock of geese flying northward attracted his attention and 'granny' told him that far beyond the hills . . . lay a northern country, where all were free." This vision caught Jones's imagination and would inspire him to find that mystical land someday.

Born in Leesburg, Virginia on June 22, 1817, Jones grew up on the plantation of the Elzy family. His father had been sold before he was born, and they never met. He was close to his mother and his maternal grandmother. From a young age, Jones worked as a domestic servant in the house and garden. There, he grew fond of the mistress of the plantation, Miss Sally Elzy, who treated him well.

As Miss Elzy aged, Jones and his family grew concerned about what would happen to the plantation—and themselves—when the kind old lady died. The young slave who harbored visions of freedom decided not to take his chances on new owners and determined to flee.

In the summer of 1844, Jones made his escape with two of his half-brothers. Leaving the plantation ostensibly for a party, the young men travelled mostly at night. With food enough for a few days, the party—now numbering five, with the addition of a couple slaves from a nearby plantation—was well armed. "John wore in his belt the best carving knife of Miss Elzy, the only thing he had ever taken from her." Each of the men carried a knife and gun.

As it turned out, the pistols helped ensure safety on the flight to freedom.

OPPOSITE: According to the website for the John W. Jones Museum: "John W. Jones' house in Elmira, New York, is an interactive museum commemorating the life and work of the former slave, who as an Underground Railroad Station Master, safely assisted nearly 800 slaves' flight to Canada and was responsible for the dignified burial of nearly 3000 Confederate soldiers." The museum is a 501(c)3 nonprofit. (cm)

John W. Jones, sexton of Woodlawn Cemetery, was an active conductor on the Underground Railroad. (tf)

While in Maryland, slave catchers apprehended the group. Brandishing their weapons, Jones and his party slipped away northward.

After crossing through the mountains of Pennsylvania, the young men were just short of the New York border when they took shelter in the barn of Dr. Nathaniel Smith in South Creek, feeling "more dead than alive." Although discovered, sympathetic hands delivered much needed sustenance, and the group rested before crossing into New York.

Arriving in Elmira in early July, Jones settled down to make some money before moving on. Within days of arriving, he made fifty cents cutting wood for Mrs. Culp; soon after, he worked for Seth Kelly, making tallow candles in Kelly's shop. Finding a welcoming and kind population in Elmira, Jones decided to make his home there, instead of moving on. Undoubtedly, the acquaintance of Judge Ariel Thurston had much to do with this decision. One among a substantial group of abolitionists, Thurston helped to secure schooling and a stable job for Jones.

While boarding with Thurston's family, Jones became custodian of Clara Thurston's girls' academy. Apparently, Jones earned the trust and respect of the folks in the community because just a few years later they appointed him sexton of the First Baptist Church. When a new church opened its doors in 1848, Jones continued to serve the new facility, remaining in the position for the next 40 years.

Shortly after John Jones arrived in Elmira he began an effort to assist runaway slaves on their own journey to freedom. Working with William Still, the primary conductor of the Underground Railroad in Philadelphia, Jones began sheltering and guiding runaways on their way to Canada—sometimes as many as 30 at a time.

Born a free man in Burlington, New Jersey, Still was the son of former slaves Levin and Sidney Still. About the time of the Mexican War, Still went to work for the Pennsylvania Society for the Abolition of Slavery in Philadelphia. Soon after, Still began spiriting runaways northward. With Jones's help, Elmira became an important station on the Underground Railroad.

Judge Ariel Thurston mentored John Jones and was a passionate abolitionist. (cchs)

The passage of the Fugitive Slave Act of 1850 galvanized Jones and friends, who swore to resist the unjust law. When a committee formed to organize the resistance, they elected Jones to the secretary position. Soon after, *The Liberator*—a leading abolitionist newspaper—printed the following:

> *Resolved, That we, the colored citizens of Elmira, do hereby form ourselves into a society for the purpose of protecting ourselves against those persons, [slave-catchers] prowling through different parts of this and other States since the passing of the diabolical act of Sept. 18th, 1850, which consigns freemen of other States to that awful state of brutality which the fiendish slaveholders of the Southern States think desirable for their colored brethren, but are not willing to try it themselves.*

Reverend Thomas Beecher, an important ally in the abolitionist cause, became a close friend of John and his brother, George. In fact, George later served as the sexton of Beecher's church. Beecher, son of a prominent New England family of clerics, arrived in 1854 and became pastor of the Independent Congregational Church, later known as Park Church. Beecher could always be counted on to lend assistance to runaways and gave generously to funds used to move them along to Canada.

About 1858, Jones and his wife Rachel Swales purchased a small yellow house on a lot near the new First Baptist Church. That house soon became the hub of Underground Railroad activity in the Elmira area. According to Arch Merrill, "Jones had many allies in Elmira. Mrs. John Culp hid runaways in her home. Other Underground leaders were Jervis Langdon; Simeon Benjamin, the founder of Elmira College; Thomas Stanley Day; S. G. Andrus; John Selover; Riggs Watrous and others."

Rachel Swales married John Jones in 1856. Born in Pennsylvania in 1836, Swales was the daughter of Peter and Johanna Atkins. She and Jones had four children together: a girl and three boys—Ida Alice, born in 1857; John, 1859; George, 1861; and James, 1863.

A vital part of the Elmira community, Jones actively worked with the YMCA and assisted the volunteer fire department. If there was a fire, Jones rang the bell of the church to bring out the volunteers. He was so dedicated that he had a rope run between the bell and his bedpost, for quick action. He promoted education for African-Americans and occasionally helped to teach reading and writing.

In 1859, Jones became sexton of the new Woodlawn Cemetery located two miles north of town when it became obvious that the existing cemeteries were running out of room; since he had taken care of all the churches' cemeteries in town, he transitioned to his new duties at the new burial ground. Keeping with Victorian sensibilities, the new burial ground was consistent with the themes of the rural cemetery movement—a beautifully landscaped park-like setting with plenty of trees and pleasant walks. A noted architect, Howard Daniels designed Woodlawn Cemetery. The community dedicated

the new 100-acre site on October 9, and Jones himself dug the first grave.

When Elmira became home to a prisoner of war camp in the summer of 1864, the post commander, Lt. Col. Seth Eastman, leased land at Woodlawn to inter those prisoners who expired at the camp. The military contracted Jones to conduct the burials at $2.50 each. In time, Jones reaped over $7,000 from the unfortunate work.

Inside the stockade, a dead house was established, and the deceased lay in this makeshift building until they could be transported to the cemetery. The dead house was located between Foster's Pond and the Chemung River, in what the prisoners often called the "trans-Mississippi department." Eventually, the smallpox hospital stood nearby.

Details of prisoners placed the bodies inside pine coffins and loaded them nine deep into a

A hillside grave at Woodlawn Cemetery where John Jones worked as sexton. (ddm)

From his house, Jones could look across the street to the cemetery where he worked as sextant. (tf)

wagon for transport to Woodlawn. They carefully recorded the identity of the deceased inside and on the outside of each coffin.

Upon arrival at the cemetery, Jones personally supervised every aspect of burial. Trenches dug in advance received the coffins, placed side by side before being covered by earth. Jones kept careful records of those interred, copied into a record book from the information on the coffin. Every grave was marked by a wooden headstone; name, rank, regiment, state, and date of death were all recorded. For an added measure of record-keeping, a corked glass bottle accompanied each body, tucked in the armpit of the deceased. Inside the bottle, a sheet of paper contained all the information about that soldier.

Serving on burial detail provided employment

BETWEEN JULY 1864 AND AUGUST 1865, 2973 CONFEDERATE SOLDIERS WERE BURIED HERE WITH KINDNESS AND RESPECT, BY JOHN W. JONES, A RUNAWAY SLAVE. THEY HAVE REMAINED IN THESE HALLOWED GROUNDS OF WOODLAWN NATIONAL CEMETERY BY FAMILY CHOICE BECAUSE OF THE HONORABLE WAY IN WHICH THEY WERE LAID TO REST BY A CARING MAN.

A monument next to the Confederate section of Woodlawn National Cemetery shares the story of Jones's work tending to the dead POWs. (cm)

for prisoners, who received five cents a day and extra rations. It was heavy labor, and Mother Nature did not always make it easy. After the middle of October, the ground froze, making digging difficult. And often times, according to prisoner James Marion Howard, 12th Alabama, "Where we buried our dead we had to take a pick and make a hole in the coffin on each side near the shoulders so as to sink the dead," as the water would stand in the trenches many feet deep.

John R. Rollins's burial particularly affected Jones. When the young Confederate arrived for interment, Jones wondered if he could be the son of the Elzy plantation overseer he once knew down in Virginia. After a time, he confirmed the melancholy fact that it was the same Rollins he had known as a toddler. The family could at least be consoled that the young man had been buried with friendly hands.

After the war, Jones continued his work as church and cemetery sexton. With the profits of his many years of hard work, he purchased the 11-

Jones's house circa 1901 had a gate and posts out front. (cchs)

Carte de visite of John W. Jones about the time of his retirement in 1890. (cchs)

acre farm near Woodlawn Cemetery on College Avenue. The house he had lived in next to the Baptist Church was sold to a new owner and torn down. The Jones's family farmhouse was built in 1870; during construction, they used parts of buildings that had been part of the POW camp and perhaps a former officer's quarters.

Upon the completion of a new brick church in 1890, Jones retired from his long service to the First Baptist Church. According to Clay Holmes, "John Jones was loved by everyone in the church, old and young. He saw little girls grow up to be mothers and grandmothers." His kind smile and warm aspect drew people to him. As a reward for his faithful service, his friends presented him with a large new chair, a tribute in his honor.

Generally in good health, Jones became frailer in his 70s and suffered from heart disease. In the fall of 1900, he was wracked with pneumonia and grew weak. On the day after Christmas, Jones died at the age of 83 and was buried in Woodlawn Cemetery. Rachel survived Jones, dying in Owego, New York in 1919.

Today, the Jones house is preserved as a museum at 1250 Davis Street. Saved from demolition in the twentieth century, the house has

twice been moved, though it still stands on the original property. A group of concerned citizens formed a nonprofit organization to preserve and restore the house to its original appearance. It is now open to the public and is listed on the National Register of Historic Places.

Although the John W. Jones house has been moved, the building remains on the original Jones property. (cm)

The portion of Woodlawn Cemetery where Confederate prisoners are buried became a national cemetery in December 1877 when the U.S. government purchased the land for $1,500. The original leased half-acre had grown to a two-and-a-half-acre space by the time the last inmate was buried. After its new designation, bodies of Union soldiers buried in other sections of Woodlawn were disinterred and moved into the national cemetery. They were buried in two rows on the north side. In time, all of the wooden grave markers were replaced with marble stones.

Because of Jones's meticulous record-keeping and insistence upon a dignified burial for all, Woodlawn National Cemetery serves us as an important reminder that Americans once went

The interior of the John W. Jones house features exhibits and displays that tell Jones's story. Many of the timbers in the house are from old prison camp buildings. (ddm)

to war with each other. The peaceful field of green and marble at the cemetery is as much a testament to the kindness and care of Jones as it is a place of rest for the former Confederates now slumbering far from home—a fitting memorial for a former slave who helped others in their quests for freedom.

John Jones and his family are buried in Woodlawn Cemetery.
Their plot is tended as a memorial garden. (ddm)

A "Most Appalling" Scene
The Shohola Train Wreck of 1864

APPENDIX C
BY TERRIANNE K. SCHULTE

"Sadly familiar as the last three years have rendered the country and the public with tales of blood, scenes of slaughter, and the accumulated horrors of the battle-field, we are not yet so used to them as to feel unmoved when, on a smaller scale, some fearful railroad catastrophe brings them to us, face to face, amid the quiet of civil life." — New York Tribune, *July 18, 1864*

On July 12, 1864, hundreds of Confederate prisoners of war were sent from Point Lookout, Maryland, on the Potomac River, to the newly established prison camp at Elmira, New York. Three days later, scores of captured rebels, who had recently escaped death on the battlefield at Cold Harbor, Virginia, perished in a fiery train crash near the small town of Shohola, Pennsylvania. It marked one of the worst railroad disasters in Pennsylvania history.

This particular journey to Elmira prison, one of several that had begun earlier in the month, included 833 Confederate prisoners, 125 Union guards, and 3 commissioned officers from the 11th and 20th Regiment Veteran Reserve Corps under the command of Capt. Morris H. Church. On Thursday, July 14, the prisoners reached New York City from Point Lookout aboard the steamer *Crescent* at three o'clock in the afternoon, finally arriving in Jersey City, New Jersey, early the next morning. The soldiers then boarded an 18-car "extra" train—Engine 171—that included a few boxcars and mostly passenger coaches.

As an "extra," Engine 171 was supposed to follow the scheduled West 23 train for the 273-mile journey, but they fell an hour behind schedule after a few prisoners tried to escape and were subsequently captured.

At 6 a.m. on Friday, July 15, the Confederates departed for Elmira, two hours after they had arrived in Jersey City. To make matters worse, Engine 171 also waited for a drawbridge along the route. But West 23 carried flags to indicate that there was an "extra" train following it, and so the prisoner train should have been accorded the right-of-way, even though it was running late.

A blind curve at the crash site made it impossible for the speeding locomotives to see each other. (HMBD/Scott J. Payne)

The Erie Railway depot at Shohola Station stood at Rohman Avenue and Richardson Street in Shohola, Pike County, Pennsylvania.
(cchs)

Around 1 p.m., Engine 171 briefly stopped in Port Jervis, Pennsylvania, for additional wood fuel and water. A reporter for the *New York Tribune* mentioned that "the convoy reached Port Jervis in the best of spirits," an odd way to describe the mood of captured rebels en route to a prison camp. By this point, however, Engine 171, traveling roughly 25 miles an hour, puffed along, already four hours behind schedule.

From Port Jervis westward, the mostly single track of the Erie Railroad ran along the Delaware River, twisting and turning in a succession of sharp curves through the Pocono Mountains of northeastern Pennsylvania, where visibility was often reduced to a hundred yards or less. Fifty minutes after departing Port Jervis, Engine 171 traveled 19 miles and passed through the town of Shohola. Unbeknownst to the driver of the POW train, a 50-car coal train travelled east from Lackawaxen Junction toward Port Jervis, heading directly toward them.

Shortly before 3 p.m., at King and Fuller's cut, a blind curve two miles west of Shohola, the 18-car prisoner train collided head-on with the coal train. Forty prisoners and 14 guards died instantly, with the engineer and fireman of Engine 171 buried by the wood used for fueling the POW train. Of the 37 men in the first passenger car, only

one survived "by falling between the platforms to the earth."

Prior to impact, two Union soldiers had been posted at each of the doors to the cars. Some Confederate prisoners had also been standing on the platforms talking with the guards when the accident occurred. "Of the men thus standing," the *New York Tribune* reported, "all were immediately killed," with the exception of just a few fortunate individuals. Shortly after the crash, three Union guards and eight Confederate prisoners died from their wounds as well.

Survivors interviewed by the *New York Tribune* in the wake of the crash reported a "most appalling" scene:

> the road [was] blocked up with debris, car piled upon car in the most indescribable confusion, the bodies of those thrown from them covering the road at every step, the flying dust and blinding smoke from the quenching fires, the noise of the escaping steam, and, above all, the fearful groans and heart rending cries of the injured and expiring will never be forgotten.

Evoking images of apocalyptic horror, battle-scarred veterans described how

Steam engine, circa 1860, similar to model carrying coal which collided with a troop train near Shohola, PA. (loc)

[s]ome of the corpses were shockingly mutilated, heads completely crushed, bodies transfixed, impaled on timbers or iron rods, or smashed between the colliding beams, while one man was discovered dead, sitting on the top of the upturned tender, in grotesque and ghastly mockery of the scene around him.

Immediately after the accident, the survivors began the grisly task of removing the injured and the dead from the wreckage. While the sound of the crash was "eerily muffled by the sharply rising mountains on both sides of the railroad track," the timely arrival of residents from Shohola and nearby Barryville, New York, provided much-needed assistance to the wounded and significantly helped with the recovery efforts. Injured soldiers, and those who had managed to escape unharmed, were quickly transported to the nearby Shohola train station and the Shohola Glen Hotel.

John Vogt, who lived near the scene of the accident, recalled how his "home was stripped of everything that could be made into bandages for the injured and blankets and bedding and clothing were also utilized." Meanwhile, the superintendent of the Erie Railroad, Hugh Riddle, sent doctors and additional railroad workers to the scene of the crash to aid in the rescue operations.

Capitalizing on the confusion at the crash site, five Confederates managed to escape and were never captured, despite Captain Church's efforts to post guards at the site "immediately" after the crash. An elderly woman interviewed years after the event recalled that as a young girl she had encountered two of the men who appeared to be "escaping prisoners," as she and a friend headed to the accident site.

While the wounded were cared for, attention shifted to those who had not survived the crash. Years later, Vogt described how his yard was transformed into a temporary morgue until the morning of Saturday, July 16, when the dead were hastily buried in a 6-foot-deep trench measuring 76 feet in length and 8 feet wide dug "below the steep bluff into the swamp on the second bank of the Delaware River." Four Confederates lay in each coffin, which had been swiftly constructed utilizing salvaged wood from the wreckage. Each deceased Union guard, however,

A monument to the Shohola victims, erected in 1912, stands next to the Confederate section of Woodlawn National Cemetery. (cchs)

rested in a single coffin. They remained there in the makeshift cemetery undisturbed for the next 47 years. Two Confederates who died shortly after the accident were buried in the Congregational Cemetery in Barryville, New York, a neighboring community directly across the river from Shohola. At 11 a.m. on the 16th, the remaining prisoners who were well enough to travel departed for Elmira, arriving at 9:30 that night. One long terrifying journey had ended. A new and equally terrifying experience began.

So ultimately the question becomes, why were eastbound and westbound trains sharing a single track and therefore destined to collide? Many have argued that Douglas "Duff" Kent, an alcoholic telegraph operator in Lackawaxen, Pennsylvania, had apparently sealed the fate of those aboard the POW and coal trains. Several accounts claimed that Kent had been out drinking the night before the wreck and continued drinking on the fateful day. Writing in the *Pike County (Pennsylvania) Dispatch* almost a hundred years later, D. Nelson Raynor said that when the conductor of the coal train, John Martin, asked Kent if the road was clear for them to proceed, Kent, "under the influence of liquor at his post," apparently forgot about the prisoner train and told him the road was clear.

Adding to the narrative regarding the culpability of "Duff" Kent, a number of newspapers in the early twentieth century also reprinted in modified form and without acknowledgement a

Originally built in 1949, the "Shohola Caboose" serves as a railroad museum and tourist center, operated by the Shohola Railroad & Historical Society. (HMDB/Bill Coughlin)

story recounted in 1911 by Edward Harold Mott in *Between the Ocean and the Lakes: The Story of Erie,* which outlined Kent's whereabouts after the wreck. "Kent was not molested," according to Mott, "but on the very night following the accident, and while scores of his victims lay dead, and scores more were writhing in agony, he attended a ball at Hawley, and danced until daylight. Next day, however, he disappeared, the voice of popular indignation becoming ominous, and he never was seen or heard of in that locality again." Although most accounts place the blame for the disaster squarely on Kent, an inquest held shortly after the accident ultimately exonerated all involved, including Kent.

In 1909, local newspapers lamented the fact that there was no official acknowledgement of the tragedy that occurred in Shohola during the summer of 1864. They observed that "all over the country historic scenes are being converted into parks and monuments . . . but how few of us realize that only twenty miles away, near the village of Shohola, nearly a hundred heroes of the great Civil War, lie in unmarked graves with only a few people knowing the exact spot and with the brush and vines growing thickly over it, save from an occasional cutting by a

CIVIL WAR PRISON TRAIN WRECK

On July 15, 1864, an Erie Railroad train carrying 833 Confederate prisoners and 128 Union guards to the prison camp at Elmira, N. Y., collided with a coal train between Shohola and Lackawaxen. About 48 prisoners and 17 guards were killed. Survivors, both injured and uninjured, were brought to Shohola where they were generously cared for by residents of the village.

PENNSYLVANIA HISTORICAL AND MUSEUM COMMISSION   1993

grand army veteran." Reflecting the post-Civil War culture of reconciliation, the paper noted that all who died there—including Confederates—"were heroes and like many sons of the north, who sleep in unknown graves on the southern battlefields, they too sleep on, utterly forgotten by the people of this section and by the thousands who annually pass by on the Erie Railroad, within a stone's throw of the scene." Some believed that occasional flooding of the Delaware over the years had already carried off many of the bodies, although John Vogt, who lived near the accident site, and had witnessed the grisly scene over four decades earlier, maintained that the graves remained untouched. Burial records, however, showed that "only sixty remains" were recovered in 1911, when the federal government disinterred the bodies and transferred them to Woodlawn National Cemetery in Elmira. So, "it was very likely," as Michael Gray suggests in his book on Elmira prison, "that Delaware River floods had washed some away."

On May 27, 1912, the "Shohola Monument" erected at Woodlawn National Cemetery memorialized those who were killed in the crash. The north side of the monument recognized

In 1993, Pennsylvania erected a state historical marker to tell the story of the accident.
(HMDB/Bill Coughlin)

the Union guards, and the south side listed the Confederate prisoners. A historical marker was also erected on route 434 in Shohola, Pennsylvania, on September 1, 1993, to acknowledge the calamity that occurred there on the fateful afternoon of July 15, 1864. Over 150 years later, the Shohola train wreck remains one of the worst railroad disasters in Pennsylvania history.

The monument's plaque bearing the names of the Confederate victims faces the Confederate section of Woodlawn National Cemetery (above). The plaque bearing the names of the Federal victims faces the Federal section of the cemetery (opposite). (cm) (cm)

DR. TERRIANNE SCHULTE *is an associate professor of history at D'Youville College in Buffalo, NY.*

Corporal Berry Benson, 1st South Carolina Infantry. (cchs)

Yours truly:
Berry Benson -
Sgt. Co. A. McGowan's Batt. Shar

APPENDIX D

BY KEVIN R. PAWLAK AND KRISTEN M. PAWLAK

On the cool and rainy evening of May 16, 1864, a 21-year-old Confederate prisoner followed an enemy guard through an oak wood near the Federal lines by Spotsylvania Court House, Virginia. Roughly 10 yards to the prisoner's right stood several lone horses—a perfect opportunity to escape, gather needed intelligence, and return safely to his unit to report his findings. As the guard stepped in front of him, the prisoner knocked down his rifle and bolted to the horses. "Halt! Halt!" yelled the guard. "Stop that man! Stop that man!" As the prisoner continued through the woods with Federal soldiers just several paces behind, on "came a party of armed men running, who caught me and held me fast." The chase ended. The Rebel soldier was captured.

The Confederate prisoner described here was Corp. Berry Benson, a combat veteran with the 1st South Carolina. Benson served in every major engagement with the Army of Northern Virginia until his capture at Spotsylvania. As one of the first soldiers to enlist in the 1st South Carolina, Benson helped Confederate forces during the firing on Fort Sumter. His devoted allegiance to the Confederacy was tested when his leg was smashed by a bullet at Chancellorsville. Yet he managed to recover and return to the front lines with his unit by the winter of 1863. The remainder of the war for Benson, though, would be the ultimate test of his resolve, forced to first survive the bloody battles of the Overland Campaign and then the northern prison camps.

Days after his capture, Benson avoided trial and execution, but got transported north to Point Lookout Prison at the mouth of the Potomac River. Roughly 10 acres in size, Point Lookout confined about 10,000 Confederate prisoners at the time of Benson's arrival. Just like his capture at Spotsylvania, Benson first looked for a way out. "It was to the sea that I turned my attention as the best avenue of escape," he recalled. "But to fit myself I should have to perfect my swimming." Benson waited for the prime opportunity.

On the evening of May 25, the second day of his captivity, Benson slipped past the guards, swam along the Potomac River, and arrived back in

These Confederate prisoners from Spotsylvania suffered the same fate as Berry Benson. (loc)

Virginia. However, just days later, Federal troops occupying northern Virginia captured him again and imprisoned him at the Old Capitol Prison in Washington, D.C. Following the battle of Fort Stevens on July 11 and July 12, Benson and other prisoners were transferred to Elmira Prison.

On July 24, after nearly two weeks on a train of freight cars, the Confederate prisoners arrived at Elmira and marched through the streets of the town to the prison. After roll call, Benson, along with two other prisoners, were "assigned to the same long room with bunks fitted up on both sides, in two rows. The bunks were made of un-planed pine boards, and as we had no blankets, they were left bare." Unlike other Federal prisons, Elmira housed its prisoners in wooden buildings instead of tents.

From the time Berry Benson passed through the wooden fence surrounding the prison camp at Elmira, he yearned to escape again and be free. Having already freed himself from the confines of one Federal prison pen, Benson began searching for clues and hints that might aid his run for freedom. A tree with branches outstretched beyond the prison walls offered one prospect; a scattered ladder ready for hasty assembly another. Benson and two fellow prisoners even crafted a desperate plan that involved recruiting followers, seizing the guards' guns from the prison arsenal, and breaking out by force.

The imprisoned South Carolinian's first plot to escape that amounted to more than delusions and dreams likewise never got off the ground. Benson and a Sergeant Hood of his regiment determined to swim across a pool within the prison walls under cover of night, work their way towards the wall on their stomachs, and dig a hole underneath the wall to break out. Moonlight illuminated enough of the camp to make the attempt that predetermined night dangerous. Hood and Benson agreed to wait for a more favorable evening. However, the "very next night," the prison guards erected large lights that lit up the inside of the camp "so that the prison was like a gas-lit sidewalk."

Tunneling seemed to be Benson's best way of absconding from the clutches of Elmira. Shortly after arriving within Elmira's walls, Benson recruited some of his friends from the Confederate army likewise held under guard to join him in a bid to dig his way out. Using his barracks as a launchpad, Benson went to work. He and his mates began digging underneath the barracks, vainly hoping to complete the 80-foot shaft quickly. Just a few days into the project, work halted.

Word reached Benson of another band of tunnelers also trying to burrow their way out. Benson met with Joe Womack of the Hampton Legion to discuss their projects. During the conversation, Womack convinced Berry that the two groups should combine their efforts and focus on one tunnel. One tunnel excavated by many people could be completed faster than two tunnels by smaller groups, Womack reasoned. Additionally, if the Federals discovered one tunnel, they would likely find the other, too. Benson agreed, and the collaboration commenced to finish Womack's tunnel.

The relationship between Womack and Benson was close. They and their crews worked fast. After three nights of tunneling, though, the group

This Confederate prisoner was photographed while at Point Lookout, the site of Berry Benson's first prison escape. (loc)

discovered other nearby tunnels. The disparate groups met again before deciding to complete two of the three tunnels. Those two were to be completed concurrently, facilitating escape through two passageways.

Little did the tunnelers know that Sgt. Melvin Mott Conklin, a Federal soldier disguised as a Confederate prisoner while working for the camp bosses, reported the tunnels. The Federals supposedly drove stakes into the tunnels, Benson learned. Yearning for freedom, he could not believe it. On August 28, 1864, Berry crawled to the tunnel's end, only to find the rumor just that. No stakes prevented further digging. Smelling freedom and sensing that time was running out, Berry worked through the night to complete the project. Two other tunnelers working alongside Benson dug through the soil to the surface by 2 a.m., August 29, but found that the escape hole was still within the prison's boundaries. The two other diggers, unaware of Benson's proximity to them, talked about finishing the work and escaping the next night if the tunnel was not discovered. If it was, said one voice in the darkness, he had another ongoing tunnel project that they could use. "You'll know me by this," said the voice to the second man.

While the darkness blocked Berry's vision of what "this" meant, he quickly cycled through the mental rolodex of fellow prisoners he had seen around the tunnel operations. Suddenly, it hit him. He often saw a man near the tunnelers with an inch-long nail on his left-hand pinky finger. Berry surmised that the man with the long nail had his partner in the dark feel that long nail. The next day, the prison guards collapsed the tunnel that Benson had dug nocturnally.

Still longing for freedom, Benson wandered the camp looking for the man with the long nail on his left hand—"my Chinese friend" to Benson. One day, Benson finally found him by the camp's water source, covertly dropping stones into the pool. Berry approached the man. Seeing through his smokescreen (the rocks came from the man's tunnel),

Benson accepted the invitation to participate in this latest underground enterprise.

Benson's "Chinese friend" was, in fact, an Alabama artillerist named Washington Traweek. Sworn to secrecy, Benson began working with the Alabamians. The newest tunnel in Berry's digging career had been underway since before the Federals foiled his last endeavor, begun on August 24.

Traweek's tunnel was positioned in a tent close to the prison's northeast corner. The diggers estimated they needed to tunnel 50-60 feet to make it beyond the wall. Immediately, Benson, by this point an experienced tunneler, noted the prospects of this project. Its entrance "was a pit about waist deep and between 2 and 2 ½ feet square." He continued: "Its entrance was a great improvement on that of the one I had started, for I had begun mine by slanting it down to the proper depth, and it was hard to back out of it. But as this one began with a perpendicular shaft, all one had to do was to straighten himself up when he got in the shaft." Perhaps more desperate than ever to escape, Benson went to work.

The seasoned Benson quickly became a great asset to Traweek's group. They "found him to be one of our best workers," remembered a cohort. Berry instituted new ideas into the process that made the work easier. Traweek's crew worked mostly during the day, not night. The hubbub of the camp covered up much of the noise coming from the tunnel. The backbreaking and suffocating work pressed on. By October 5, 1864, the tunnel's completed state allowed them to schedule an attempt for the next night.

Benson spent October 6 gathering his scant belongings for the trip to freedom. In his mind, he was already heading back to rejoin Robert E. Lee's Army of Northern Virginia. At 10 p.m., Traweek and Benson put the finishing touches on the tunnel. In pairs, the 10 men quietly began their breakout.

Berry Benson's turn came towards the end. As he had done so many times, he crawled to the tunnel's end, this time poking his head above ground outside of the camp's walls to survey the situation. The tunnel exit conveniently brought the confined prisoners above ground underneath the guard platform on the outside of the wall. Benson heard footsteps above him and saw a crowd of soldiers across the street from his location. Soon, he would have to partake on the most dangerous part of his journey—leaving the cover of the platform in full view of the soldiers standing on it. "I felt every moment that I would hear a shot and feel a bullet pierce my back," he wrote. But no shots nor shouts of "Halt!" greeted him. Benson was a free man.

After putting distance between himself and his former prison, Benson searched about for his fellow escapees at the prearranged meeting place. He called for them several times but no answers greeted his query. From the abandoned rendezvous, Benson followed the Chemung River west to Corning, where a bridge brought him to the river's south bank. Now, Benson proceeded south, yearning to rejoin the Army of Northern Virginia.

During the early portion of Benson's journey, he traversed the northern countryside day and night, liberally foraging from the farms and residences he passed. He crossed into Pennsylvania on October 10, drained from lack of sleep. Berry continued on foot, eventually reaching Williamsport, Pennsylvania, several days later. From there, he boated for a time along the Susquehanna River and walked to Northumberland, a rail depot in central Pennsylvania. He hopped onto a train and secured passage to York, using the fake story of having a dying sister there to secure a seat. Now, covering a lot of ground fast, Benson crossed the Mason-Dixon Line on October 15.

Passing through Baltimore, Berry crossed the Potomac on October 19. Eight days later, Benson encountered a Confederate patrol in Northern Virginia under command of Gen. Bradley Johnson. Johnson's patrol ushered Benson to their general's tent, where Benson ate his share of food and graced Johnson with his incredible story. Johnson presented Berry with a pass to travel to

Jubal Early's headquarters at New Market in the Shenandoah Valley. From there, Benson traveled through Richmond and ultimately to the front lines at Petersburg.

When Berry Benson arrived at the camp of his South Carolina unit and trudged through the row of tents, his stunned comrades repeatedly questioned, "Isn't that Berry Benson?" When Blackwood, Berry's brother, saw him, he asked, "When were you exchanged?" The proud Benson replied, "I wasn't exchanged, I escaped."

Just like that, Berry Benson was back in the Confederate ranks. He remained until the very end, surrendering with the Army of Northern Virginia at Appomattox Courthouse.

KEVIN PAWLAK *is a historic site manager for the Prince William County Historic Preservation Division.*

KRISTEN PAWLAK *is on staff at the Missouri Civil War Museum.*

Both are regular contributors to Emerging Civil War.

"A Foretaste of Heaven"
How Elmira Gave the World Mark Twain

APPENDIX E
BY R. MICHAEL GOSSELIN

The first thing a visitor sees after driving through the Walnut Street gates of Woodlawn Cemetery in Elmira is a small, green sign that reads, "MARK TWAIN NEXT RIGHT." It is impossible to get lost after that. More signs lead up a hill—straight past the grave of John W. Jones—to a modest stone, occasionally sprinkled with cigars and pennies, that reads:

Samuel Langhorne Clemens
MARK TWAIN
Nov. 30, 1835 – Apr. 21, 1910

Elmira is, in the words of the website, *Mark Twain Country*, "Where Twain Remains." The grave is not his only imprint on the city, though. There's also a Mark Twain Motor Inn, Mark Twain Riverfront Park, and Mark Twain Golf Course, plus, in previous years, a Tom Sawyer Motor Inn, Mark Twain Hotel (with a Tom Sawyer room), Huck Finn Soda Bar, Connecticut Yankee Room, Mark Twain Men's Shop, and Mark Twain Gown Shoppe. Sam Clemens's influence on Elmira seems obvious. But what was the city's influence on him? In a word, it was profound, and most of it due to his wife's family.

For someone born in 1835, Clemens's early life was surprisingly distant from the political issues of the day. He piloted steamboats during the 1850s, spent the Civil War years in Nevada, California, and Hawaii, and, in 1867, promptly set sail on a "Great Pleasure Excursion" to Europe and the Holy Land. That trip led to the publication of *The Innocents Abroad*. It also led to Livy—Olivia Langdon—whose face Clemens first saw on an ivory miniature while aboard ship. When he arrived in Elmira in August of 1868 to court her, he found himself in a city with a history of progressive activism. According to Fred Kaplan in *The Singular Mark Twain*, "Elmira had cultural and educational aspirations. A city of about sixteen thousand in 1868, it had an active Protestant elite, much of it tempered Republican by the fires of national division, with sufficient intellectual curiosity to welcome new ideas brought by magazines, books, and lecturers."

The statue of Mark Twain that stands on the campus of Elmira College is 12 feet tall from base to top—two fathoms high or, as a riverboat pilot would say, "mark twain." Designed by sculptor Gary Weisman, the statue weighs 376 pounds. (CM)

Best known for his tales of life along the Mississippi, Mark Twain was just as shaped by his own life along the Chemung. (loc)

Thanks to the railroads, it was also wealthier than it is today. The Langdon family enjoyed their place as the most prominent family in Elmira, headed by Olivia's father, Jervis, a philanthropist and social reformer. "Before and during the war," Kaplan writes, "the Langdons had combined their Christian beliefs and political views by supporting abolitionist causes. On a straight railroad run from southern Pennsylvania to the Canadian border, Elmira's citizens helped funnel runaway slaves out of the reach of federal law." They were friends with Frederick Douglass, and also supported prison reform and women's suffrage. The Langdons had left the Presbyterian Church over its refusal to condemn slavery, and, in 1846, helped to found the Independent Congregational Church, today the Park Church, at 208 W. Gray Street. In 1871, Clemens submitted a promotional piece about the Park Church to the *New York Times*, writing, "You will notice in every feature of this new church one predominant idea and purpose always discernible—the banding together of the true congregation as a family, and the making of the church a home." In a 1938 article for *Harper's Magazine*, Max Eastman wrote:

> *There was a hardier and deeper 'radicalism' in the Park Church culture into which Mark Twain married than*

there was in Mark Twain. To find so much open revolt against empty forms and conventions, so much laughing realism, and downright common sense, and democracy, and science, and reckless truth-telling in these people of Elmira who were, nevertheless, dedicated with moral courage to an ideal, may well have given Mark Twain the possession of his deepest and best self.

Thomas K. Beecher pastored the church; his brother was the famous abolitionist Henry Ward, and his sister Harriet authored *Uncle Tom's Cabin*, and Abraham Lincoln supposed said to her, "So you're the little woman who wrote the book that made this great war!" According to Eastman, Thomas Beecher was:

[t]he central figure in that Elmira, the dominant and molding intellectual and spiritual force, not only to Olivia Langdon, but in large measure to Mark Twain himself . . . a man of more than Mark Twain's stature, you must realize, in the minds of those around them . . . His thought was to live and be helpful in the community as a modern Jesus would, a downright, realistic, iconoclastic, life-loving Jesus, with a scientific training and a sense of humor and a fund of common sense.

Clemens once penned a letter to a local newspaper defending Beecher during a church scandal. The eccentric clergyman has even been credited with being the inspiration behind Clemens's fondness for white suits.

Livy brought Clemens to Elmira, of course, and they married in 1870 at the Langdon mansion, on the corner of North Main and West Church streets. (The house was demolished in 1940 and replaced with a strip mall.) Thomas Beecher performed the service.

Livy had been a social reformer long before meeting Clemens, and quickly came to influence both his conscience and his writing. According to Laura E. Trombley, in *Mark Twain in the Company of Women*, "Throughout her life, Olivia was close to women who were dynamic, intelligent, unapologetic, as well as committed feminists—women who had rejected the purely domestic sphere in favor of participation of the outside world." Kaplan writes, "Cossetted by a loving, principled family, Olivia . . . was from childhood the beneficiary of her parents' enlightened ideas and Elmira's cultural resources." Albert Bigelow Paine, editor of a 1917 edition of *Mark Twain's Letters*, said, "Olivia Langdon had a keen and refined literary instinct, and the *Innocents Abroad*, as well as Mark Twain's other books, are better to-day for her influence." Sam himself said of Livy, "I never wrote a serious word until after I married Mrs. Clemens. She is solely responsible—to her should go all the credit—for any influence my subsequent work should exert. After my marriage, she edited everything I wrote."

Of all the influences that the Langdons had on Clemens, though, perhaps Olivia's older sister, Susan, had the greatest impact. Born Susan Dean in 1836, she was adopted by the Langdons after the death of her parents, and later married Theodore Crane. "A capable, diffident, kind person," writes Kaplan, "she spent much of her time and apparently endless patience helping other people. Gradually she became as much of an intimate of Livy's husband as she had always been of her sister. Childless, she would also become a second mother to their family." Twain thought of her as an angel: "I can believe a good deal of the bible but I never will believe that a heaven can be devised that will keep Susie Crane from spending the most of her time in Hell trying to comfort the poor devils down there." When the Clemens's young daughter, Susy, died in 1896, Susan Crane was the only family member at her bedside, and the delirious girl mistook her for her mother.

From 1879-1889, Clemens and his family spent their summers at Quarry Farm, Susan Crane's property in the eastern hills overlooking Elmira. Like many other families with a cherished summer place, the Clemenses spent 20 idyllic seasons in Elmira. The summer breezes were welcome, as was a seemingly small army of cats, and the girls—Susy, Jean and Clara—must have considered it a paradise.

"The three summer months which I spend here," Clemens explained, "are usually my working months. I am free here and can work uninterruptedly . . . this may be called the home of *Huckleberry Finn* and other books of mine, for they were written here." According to Gretchen Sharlow, Director of the Elmira College Center for Mark Twain Studies, Susan and her husband "had significant influence on the life of the Clemens family and on Mark Twain as a writer . . . It was that period which biographers have characterized as being the happiest, healthiest and most productive for Mark Twain." As Clemens's niece, Dr. Ida Langdon, recalled years later, "The Farm was never lonely, never monotonous, never dull, but it was utterly quiet and undisturbed. It was a wonderful place for my uncle to work (according to him the best place anywhere in the world). It was also to him a very beautiful place, a place, he said, in which to take a foretaste of Heaven."

The company at Quarry Farm was pleasant and diverse. Clemens's early racial experiences involved growing up around slaves in Missouri, and in seeing the animosity directed at Chinese immigrants in California (whom he called, in *Roughing It*, a "kindly, well-meaning race"). Explicit denunciations of slavery are rare in his writings from those days. One such example—striking in its solitude—can be found in *The Innocents Abroad*, where, after briefly meeting a museum guide in Venice, Clemens wrote, "The guide I have spoken of is the only one we have had yet who knew any thing. He was born in South Carolina, of slave parents. They came to Venice while he was an infant . . . Negroes are deemed as good as white people, in Venice, and so this man feels no desire to go back to his native land. His judgment is correct."

Twain's octagonal study, a gift from his sister-in-law, now sits at the heart of Elmira College, which also boasts the Center for Mark Twain Studies. (CM)

At Quarry Farm, however, Clemens formed closer friendships with two of Susan Crane's staff: Mary Ann Cord and John T. Lewis. Cord, born a slave, worked as Quarry Farm's cook. In 1874, Clemens published "A True Story, Word for Word as I Heard It," a criticism of slavery, which he claimed to have written in Cord's dialect, exactly as he heard it one evening on the porch of the farm. The story begins: "It was summer time, and twilight. We were sitting on the porch of the farm-house, on the summit of the hill, and 'Aunt Rachel' was sitting respectfully below our level, on the steps,—for she was our servant, and colored." Lewis, a free African American farmer on the property, earned Twain's admiration and friendship after rescuing several Langdons from almost certain death in a carriage behind a runaway horse as they were leaving Quarry Farm. "I have not known an honester man nor a more respect-worthy one," Twain said. "Naturally I hold him in high and grateful regard."

In 1874, Susan Crane gave Clemens an octagonal

study, modeled after the pilothouse of a riverboat. The study—now on the grounds of Elmira College—originally perched on a rocky outcrop just up the hill from the farmhouse. The building and the location worked wonders. According to Trombley, "Clemens wrote his novels under carefully controlled conditions. He required two outwardly paradoxical elements: quiet isolation for concentration, and the comforting, boisterous presence of his family. He had both elements at Quarry Farm." The study is where he wrote major portions of *The Adventures of Tom Sawyer*, *Adventures of Huckleberry Finn*, *Life on the Mississippi*, *A Connecticut Yankee in King Arthur's Court*, *The Prince and the Pauper*, and *A Tramp Abroad*.

Privacy was not the only feature in the hideaway. Quarry Farm affords a sweeping—and inspiring—view of Elmira and the Chemung River, one that must have appealed to Clemens's love of landscape. In an 1874 letter to Joseph Hopkins Twitchell, he wrote:

> *Susie Crane has built the loveliest study for me, you ever saw. It is octagonal, with a peaked roof, each octagon filled with a spacious window, and it sits perched in complete isolation on top of an elevation that commands leagues of valley and city and retreating ranges of distant blue hills. It is a cosy nest, with just room in it for a sofa and a table and three or four chairs—and when the storms sweep down the remote valley and the lightning flashes above the hills beyond, and the rain beats upon the roof over my head, imagine the luxury of it!*

In later years, his daughter, Clara, recalled, "On a sunny day you could see the Chemung River sparkling far below as it wound its way through the town of Elmira, nestled cozily between the hills surrounding it. At night, the streets and houses, though at a great distance, seemed ablaze with artificial fire. It was a lovely sight."

Descriptions of faraway peaks and bejeweled, gas-lit cities feature prominently in Clemens's travel writings, such as his view of Naples in *The Innocents Abroad*, or the ecstatic, pages-long description of Mont Blanc, in *A Tramp Abroad*, which concludes with:

> *Indeed, those mighty bars of alternate light and shadow streaming up from behind that dark and prodigious form and occupying the half of the dull and opaque heavens, was the most imposing and impressive marvel I had ever looked upon. There is no simile for it, for nothing is like it. If a child had asked me what it was, I should have said, "Humble yourself, in this presence, it is the glory flowing from the hidden head of the Creator."*

MICHAEL GOSSELIN *is an associate professor of English at Genesee Community College in Batavia, NY.*

Such landscapes reveal a romantic—even spiritual—side to Clemens, too often lost in his reputation for cynical, Gilded Age realism.

There was another side to him as well, one revealed in notes he wrote in Quarry Farm's extensive library: that of a scholar and political theorist. Joe B. Fulton, in *Mark Twain in the Margins: The Quarry Farm Marginalia and A Connecticut Yankee in King Arthur's Court*, argues that the notes Clemens left in the books show an underappreciated facet of his novels—that they "unsettle the usual view of Twain as a writer whose sources were primarily personal and experiential. Twain's comments written in the margins of books that contributed to his own work surprise, even stun, long-time readers of his prose." Furthermore, "[g]iven Twain's extensive use of outside sources, and the records he kept in his writing journals, one has to question the attribution of an unconscious, psychological method of composition when the conscious forces are so readily apparent." William Dean Howells, editor of *The Atlantic Monthly* and author of *The Rise of Silas Lapham*, seems to have agreed. "It's charming, original, wonderful! good in fancy and sound to the core in morals," he wrote, after reading *Yankee*. "It seems God did not forget to put a soul into you."

Although clean in this photo, Twain's grave can often be found with cigars left on top as mementos. (cm)

God took that soul back in 1910. Twenty years after the family's last summer at Quarry Farm, Clemens died at his house in Connecticut. Livy had passed away six years earlier in Italy. Two of the girls had also died: Susy (1896) and Jean (1909), both in Connecticut. Clara lived until 1962, then passed away in California. None of them except Livy knew Elmira as their home, yet back they finally came, one by one, to be buried in the place where they had probably been the happiest in their lives, and among the Langdons, who showered them—and, ultimately, us—with their beneficence. And so, Elmira claims the remains of Sam Clemens, after helping give the world Mark Twain. It's a fair trade.

Andersonville

APPENDIX F
BY DEREK D. MAXFIELD

1864 brought with it dark clouds for the fortunes of the Confederacy and, for prisoners of war, immeasurable suffering. POW camps, Union and Confederate, were taxed to their limit already and the year's heavy fighting would cause conditions to deteriorate rapidly.

In an effort to alieve the overcrowding in Richmond prisons, Confederate authorities constructed a new prison camp—just a giant corral, really—near Andersonville, Georgia. The first Union POWs arrived in February. But the Overland Campaign, which began in May 1864, convinced Brig. Gen. John H. Winder, who oversaw the Confederate Bureau of Prison Camps, and Secretary of War James Seddon that sending POWs from the Richmond area to southern Georgia also placed them out of the reach of advancing Union armies. Unfortunately, time would also prove that placing a very large POW camp in out-of-the-way Andersonville meant that the camp would become logistically more difficult to supply the facility.

Situated in south-central Georgia about 125 miles south of Atlanta, Camp Sumter—the formal name given to the Andersonville pen—would become the most infamous of all Civil War prisoner of war camps with a death rate approaching thirty percent. It was also the largest. At its height, the Georgia pen held almost 30,000 men.

Although the original plan called for the construction of barracks on 16.5 acres, authorities quickly abandoned that idea and instead erected a double stockade with no shelters inside. The whole facility was hastily constructed and was, in fact, incomplete when the first prisoners arrived in February 1864. Prisoners were dumped in helter-skelter, with no arrangement or organization. Once inside, prisoners had to improvise.

Even after prisoners arrived, correspondence between Confederate officials makes it clear that all

Andersonville National Cemetery contains the remains of nearly 13,000 soldiers who died in the nearby prison camp. (ddm)

was not well for those in the camp or those who worked at it. "There is no market whatever at this post and it is utterly impossible that my laborers and employees can purchase the necessary food to live upon," R. B. Winder, assistant quartermaster,

complained to Commissary of Subsistence Major A. M. Allen, "except at the caprice and exorbitant charges of such persons as will bring provisions to them, and it is equally impossible for them to obtain board of any kind at any price. Under these circumstances the Quartermaster-General has instructed me to sell to them at Government rates what provisions they may require. Again, how are my negro laborers to be fed?"

For the men inside the Andersonville stockade, there was almost no shelter from the sun—but two trees in the beginning. Prisoners would seek cover from the burning Georgia sun by placing blankets on

Makeshift shelters known as "shebangs" built along the deadline were often tied to the rail fence for added stability. Reconstructed shebangs are on display inside the site of the old stockade at Andersonville National Historic Site. (cm)

sticks, improvising shelter with old tents, or even digging holes in the ground. There were no streets running through the camp, inmates plopped down wherever there was room. That became more and more difficult as new prisoners poured in. Although the facility was created to house 10,000, the inmate population quickly exceeded that number and Confederates had to construct an addition.

In July, a ten-acre add-on helped to alleviate crowding—but not for long. With a population of nearly 24,000 men before the addition, new arrivals pushed the total above 32,000 in August. Conditions deteriorated rapidly. Confederate Capt. H. M. Hammond, inspecting the camp, called it "crowded, filthy, and insecure." Because many of the prisoners had come directly from Belle Isle, they were already worn down and weak. The situation was ripe for disaster. During the month of August, men died at a rate of one hundred a day.

Disease was a serious problem at Andersonville,

as it was at all POW camps. Many prisoners arrived at the Georgia camp with smallpox and were thrown into the general population without any attempt to isolate them. Scurvy was also a significant problem, caused by poor diet. This ailment would cause bleeding, swollen gums, and loss of teeth.

But, perhaps the more devastating problem was dysentery, which is caused by bacteria that are ingested from polluted food or water. Inside the pen, the sinks were primitive and unvaulted and entirely inadequate. A stream of water ran through the center of the camp, but it was soon polluted so badly that to drink from it was an invitation to death. Fouled with fecal matter, urine, maggots, and other assorted bugs, it teemed with parasites and bacteria. Because prisoners were not furnished with adequate fresh water (though some ambitious ones dug their own wells), if they wanted water, they had few choices. The result was chronic diarrhea, dehydration, intestinal cramps, and eventually death. There was almost no way to effectively treat or cure dysentery, even if the camp surgeons had medicines, which they did not.

The men faced other small miseries, too. Although many of them brought vermin on their person when they arrived at Andersonville—lice and fleas—now they encountered chiggers. A family of mites (the scientific name is *trombiculidae*), these small red bugs are barely visible to the eye and feed on skin cells. Their bite causes intense itching and often an irritating rash. Scratching often led to open sores and infection for prisoners.

Sometimes, men met the absurdity of the situation with dark humor, such as contests where prisoners guess the number of odd or even vermin crawling over them. But the condition of some poor souls was no laughing matter. Private Charlie Mosher recalled looking with pity on a fellow prisoner who not only had "the lice and fleas feeding on him, but out of every aperture of his body the maggots were crawling."

Perhaps the greatest challenge for Wirz was feeding the prisoners in his charge. By the summer

The man most associated with Andersonville was Capt. Henry Wirz, who became commandant in late March. Born in Switzerland in 1823, Wirz came to the U.S. in 1849. Before the war, he worked as a physician and at water cure resorts; later, he managed a plantation in Louisiana. At the outset of the war, Wirz enlisted in the 4th Battalion of Louisiana Infantry. Following the first battle of Manassas, the Swiss warrior was assigned to duty in the Richmond prisons and, after a medical furlough and minor diplomatic mission to Europe, was assigned to Camp Sumter in Georgia. His imperial manner and callousness seemed ready-made for managing prisoner-of-war facilities. (wc)

of '64, the Confederacy could barely feed its own soldiers. According to historian Lonnie Speers, the rations, which were never ample, diminished rapidly after June: "First the salt went, then the sweet potato. In time the amount of cornmeal was reduced, and finally meat was totally eliminated." Sometimes, prisoners would go days at a time without being issued any rations.

Intense hunger caused grave suffering at the Georgia pen and caused men to go to great lengths to find anything to eat. As at other POW camps, the men might catch and devour rats and other varmints. At Andersonville, swallows were snatched from the air and eaten. When there was nothing to be hunted, men would eat their belts or other leather. Everything short of cannibalism seemed to reign.

Disease and starvation were not the only causes of death at Andersonville. Suicide by guard became a regular occurrence. Like other stockade camps, Andersonville had a "deadline," marked by a low rail fence, that ran around the interior perimeter of the stockade to keep inmates off the palisade. Prisoners

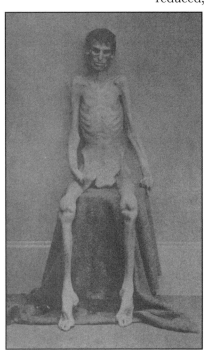

Images of emaciated prisoners, such as this unidentified Union veteran held at Belle Island, have become synonymous with Andersonville. Even in the 1880s era of reconciliation, such images did much to fuel postwar resentment on both sides about the way prisoners of war were treated. (loc)

were not allowed to cross the deadline, and guards were quick to shoot anyone who did. Eventually, this became a quick way to end it all. Driven to madness by starvation and exposure, men invited death.

A few men engineered escapes. According to the National Park Service, 351 men escaped, although most were recaptured and returned to Andersonville or sent to other prisons. Between February of 1864 and May of 1865, 32 Union soldiers successfully escaped, free and clear. "This means that 0.07%, or only one out of every 1,400 prisoners held at Andersonville successfully escaped," the Park Service says.

When Union Maj. Gen. William Tecumseh Sherman launched his Atlanta Campaign and bore down on Atlanta, Confederate authorities, fearing a Union raid, were anxious to move the prisoners from Camp Sumter. By the time Sherman captured Atlanta in September, most prisoners had been moved out—under the pretense of exchange. Sadly, almost 10,000 remained in the pen because they were too weak to travel. Most of these unfortunates would die before winter.

Word of the condition of prisoners at Andersonville spread northward in the summer and fall, sometimes from the accounts of those who had escaped, and a furor erupted in the North. The Confederacy was accused of deliberately starving and torturing Union prisoners. A bombshell report from a committee of the U.S. House of Representatives in late spring 1864 confirmed the worst. Supplemented by "images of emaciated captives," the House committee argued that "the evidence proves a determination on the part of rebel authorities . . . [to adopt] a system of treatment so horrible that the survivors present literally the appearance of living skeletons . . . maimed for life." Unfortunately for Confederate prisoners of war languishing in Northern prison camps, the answer to this news was a will to retaliate by Union authorities.

Andersonville National Historical Site, run by the National Park Service, is also the home of the National Prison of War Museum. For more information, visit www.nps.gov/ande. (cm)

Andersonville closed in May 1865. The Federal government charged Wirz with war crimes and, in November, 1865, was convicted and hanged. A national cemetery remains at the site, the final resting place of some 12,000 Union dead. A former prisoner, Dorence Atwater, charged with burying many of the dead, kept private notes on the identities of those he interred. As a result, only 460 of Andersonville's graves as marked as "unknown."

Saving Hellmira

APPENDIX G
By Terri Olszowy

Elmira's Civil War legacy is being preserved by a dedicated group of volunteers under the auspices of the Friends of the Elmira Civil War Prison Camp. The undertaking initially coalesced around the period of the Confederate prisoner of war camp of 1864-65. Today, the project also addresses the history of Elmira's role as a New York State recruiting depot from 1861-62 and draft rendezvous in 1863.

Over the years since the war ended, there had been periodic attempts to record and preserve Elmira's Civil War history. Beginning with the laying of the granite blocks marking the northeast and northwest corners of the Confederate prisoner of war camp, and then the erection of a monument honoring the 107th New York by members of the Grand Army of the Republic, local citizens have attempted to document the city's experiences with varying success.

These efforts continued up into the mid-1980s when a local historian, Carl Morrell, identified a building attributed to the Civil War camp. With the help of Al Robinson, an engineer with Fagan Engineers, the building was documented, marked, disassembled, and placed in storage pending acquisition of a suitable site for reassembly. About the same time, a commemorative marker with interpretive placards was installed on the grounds within the perimeter of the camp—an effort spearheaded by a local history teacher, Jim Hare. Shortly thereafter, one of the original camp flagpoles was identified and relocated to ground near the monument. However, three decades would pass before the dream of reassembling the building was realized.

In 2015, a group of interested citizens formed the Friends of the Elmira Civil War Prison Camp. The Friends applied for and received 501(c)3 nonprofit status with the following mission and vision statements:

Appearance of the historical building as it came out of storage. (to)

At the official ground breaking ceremony: Confederate Sgt. Robert Roe; Union Capt. Douglas Oakes; and at the far right, President of FECWPC, Martin Chalk. (to)

The mission of the Friends of the Elmira Civil War Prison Camp is to protect and preserve the history of the American Civil War in Elmira, Chemung County and surrounding areas and to educate the public about that history.

Our vision is to be the primary resource for history, education and preservation of the Civil War experience for Elmira, Chemung County and the surrounding areas. This will include working cooperatively with other local groups, as well as building relationships with relevant organizations nationally.

Fundraising began for the purpose of property acquisition upon which to reconstruct the original building attributed to Barracks No. 3, which had been in storage. The Friends negotiated a land transfer of a small plot of property belonging to the City of Elmira that laid within the footprint of the original camp perimeter. The Elmira Water Board allowed the Friends to use adjacent space for reassembly, and the building was brought out of storage. At this point, the enormity of the task became all too apparent. The intervening 30-plus years between disassembly and reassembly had not been kind to the building. Poor storage and multiple moves resulted in lost and damaged materials. The tags that had been used to identify individual pieces

had deteriorated beyond use. Main structural beams had rotted and a large portion of the siding was missing, as well as half of the second-level flooring.

The Friends hauled the old building out of storage and had to piece together an intricate puzzle. (to)

Throughout the summer of 2015, Spotts Builders LLC, scores of volunteers, and several other local businesses partnered to prepare the ground and materials. Nails pulled from the building were saved, and a limited number of them were preserved in Lucite to be used for fundraising and recognition of major donors. Original wood deemed structurally unsound for reuse was also saved for future repairs and fundraising. Spotts methodically laid out the pieces and, over a period of six months, slowly pieced the jigsaw puzzle back together. A ground-breaking ceremony was conducted, and the public was apprised of the project.

2016 was a year of constant activity requiring the coordination of significant resources, and the local community delivered in a big way. Fagan Engineers and Land Surveyors donated technical expertise and site surveys. The original building was completed and moved from the temporary construction site to its permanent location by Dimon and Bacorn Inc., a local moving company. The Cornell Cooperative Extension Master Gardeners assisted in the design and installation of a memorial garden. The vegetation selected for the garden included the state flowers representing the

Left in photo, a reconstructed historical building. Its function is unknown, but it was most likely a form of utility building. Right in photo, the beginning of full-scale replica barracks building. (to)

home states of Confederate prisoners of war. The murals in the windows were produced by members of the Community Arts of Elmira.

The enthusiasm generated by the reassembly of the original building, dubbed "Building Number 1," spawned a second construction project: a full-scale barracks building replicating an early war structure originally used to house Union recruits and later occupied by prisoners of war. Using period photographs and contemporary descriptions of the structure, a local design and project firm, Barn-Livin', donated the blueprint design for construction. Building materials were sourced to provide an appearance as close as possible to original descriptions, to include true dimensional rough-cut hemlock lumber and Civil War-era-style cut nails. Again, it was through the efforts of many volunteers, supported by the staff of the Chemung County Historical Society, that the project to preserve Elmira's history moved forward.

In the spring of 2017, the Friends were ready to open the site to the public. A grand opening and dedication took place. In addition to the inclusion of the usual public dignitaries and a series of speakers, a living history event based on the arrival of the first 400 Confederate prisoners of war was presented. Juried participants recreated the march

Living historians assist FECWPC by recreating a POW work detail to help build the replica barracks building. (to)

of the prisoners along the historic route from the railroad depot to Barracks No. 3. Throughout the day, scenarios based on historical accounts were recreated, including the use of prisoner labor to help build the barracks buildings. Representatives from the Sons of Union Veterans, Sons of Confederate Veterans, Daughters of Union Veterans, and the United Daughters of the Confederacy participated in a memorial held at Woodlawn National Cemetery where deceased Confederate prisoners of war lie buried. Throughout the summer, volunteers staffed the site providing tours and orientation for the general public.

2018 saw expansion of interpretive exhibits and completion of the barracks building, which was christened Ward Thirty-Six, based on an account of a former prisoner who returned to visit Elmira after the war. Outreach to local schools resulted in the development of school programming. A summer lecture series, History Under the Trees, was offered to the public. Presentations touched on topics relevant to Elmira, including military punishment practices, Civil War-era medicine, and the saga of a local Union soldier who survived combat, prison, and the sinking of his troop transport ship in the Atlantic on the way home. Representatives of the Friends continued public engagement via presentations for local organizations and historical societies.

With the completion of the construction projects, the Friends's attention turned to interior projects in 2019. Volunteers continued to expand educational and research opportunities. The organization reached out to Cornell University and the Chemung County Historical Society to assist with the creation of a research library and archives. Capriotti Properties provided the Friends a physical location for their operations in the antebellum Foster House. The owner of the house during the Civil War, William Foster, leased the grounds for Barracks No. 3 to the U.S. government and was located almost directly across the street from the main gate of the prison compound. Originally, the house consisted of just the center section between four chimneys. Additions on either side were constructed well after the war, and expansion in the rear of the building continued into the twentieth century when the home was converted into medical offices.

A memorial garden showcases the state flower of each state Confederate POWs belonged to. (to)

The Friends of the Elmira Civil War Prison are excited about the opportunities for future expansion and development of the site. Volunteerism forms the bedrock of the organization's success, and volunteers are always enthusiastically welcomed. Pursuit of partnerships with local, state, and national research repositories will aid in the enhancement of the understanding of Elmira's role during the war and its effect on the community. Planned projects for the future include:

- Installation of wrought iron fencing
- Installation of external interpretive markers

Living historians forming to retrace the footsteps of the first 400 Confederate POWs accompanied by their Union guards from the Erie railroad station to Barracks No. 3. (to)

· Establishment of an annual symposium
· Acquisition of primary source documentation
· Launching of a research library
· Establishment of a career skills internship program
· Development of a nationally recognized "Scholar In Residence" program
· Creation of a descendants' organization
· Site expansion

The Friends continue to function as an all-volunteer organization and attribute their current success to the invaluable partnerships of both private and community supporters. Private individual and local business donations have been and will continue to be integral to the organization's ability to continue improving and delivering on the mission. Anyone interested in helping preserve Elmira's Civil War legacy is invited to visit the Friends website at www.elmiraprisoncamp.com and follow the Facebook page @Elmira Civil War Prison Camp for ways to help.

TERRI OLSZOWY *is a board member of the Friends of the Elmira Civil War Prison Camp.*

Suggested Reading

HELLMIRA

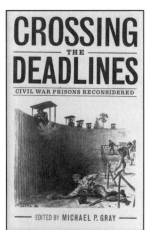

Crossing the Deadlines: Civil War Prisons Reconsidered
Edited by Michael P. Gray
The Kent State University Press (2018)
ISBN-13: 978-1606353417

This intriguing collection of essays explores the dark reaches of Civil War prison scholarship from a variety of viewpoints and professions, including historians, anthropologists and public historians. The eclectic mix of topics includes environment, race, material culture, memory and more.

The Business of Captivity: Elmira and Its Civil War Prison
Michael P. Gray
The Kent State University Press (2015)
ISBN-13: 978-1606352663

The definitive work on the Elmira POW camp, Gray's book is a captivating account of life inside the pen on the Chemung River. Especially valuable is Gray's account of Elmira's management by the post commanders, commandants, and Commissary General of Prisoners, and its supervision by the War Department. It is a web of intrigue and even conspiracy. Another important aspect of this path-breaking book is the micro-economy that was created by the prisoners, who kept themselves busy by catching and selling rats, making jewelry and other ornaments, and fostering a marketplace where tobacco was the primary medium of exchange.

Elmira: Death Camp of the North
Michael Horigan
Stackpole Books (2002)
ISBN-13: 978-0811714327

A native of Elmira, Horigan sought to uncover the grisly story of the Elmira prisoner of war camp and why it was so deadly to its inhabitants. Not only does he reveal the constellation of hardships faced by prisoners, but a story of retribution that he pins on Secretary of War Edwin Stanton, and the penny-pinching Commissary General of Prisoners, William Hoffman. In the end, Horigan lays out a damning indictment, which he carefully enumerates in his conclusion, of the conduct of the War Department and officers overseeing the Elmira camp who he blames for the great suffering and death along the banks of the Chemung River in 1864-65.

In Vinculis, or A Prisoner of War
Anthony M. Keiley
Sagwan Press (2015)
ISBN-13: 978-1340278366

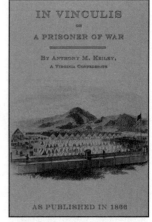

Anthony M. Keiley was a Virginia gentleman, lawyer, and member of the House of Delegates when he was captured in June of 1864 while assisting the Petersburg militia. Keiley was first sent to Point Lookout POW camp in Maryland before he was transferred to the Elmira camp in New York. Designed to hold enlisted Confederate soldiers, not officers, Keiley stood out from the common inmates. Well educated, articulate and urbane, Keiley was both discerning and ambitious. His account of his time incarcerated, originally published in 1866, has become a staple for historians studying Civil War POW camps.

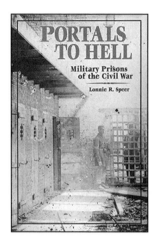

Portals to Hell: Military Prisons of the Civil War
Lonnie R. Speer
Stackpole Books (1997)
ISBN-10: 0811703347

This authoritative book is the first comprehensive study of all major Civil War prisons, North and South. Speer traces the development of the POW facilities: the various types used throughout the war from barren ground affairs to the infamous stockade—like Andersonville. We learn about the system of prisoner exchange created in the crisis and how it broke down, including how the taking of African-American prisoners ultimately spelled doom for the cartel. Speer also provided invaluable appendices that cover the language of prisons, a medical glossary, and a quick reference guide to the POW camps of both sides. This essential tool helps us categorize prisons by type, years they existed, capacity, escapes and number of deaths.

Haunted by Atrocity: Civil War Prisons in American Memory
Benjamin G. Cloyd
LSU Press (2010)
ISBN-13: 978-0807136416

One of the hottest fields of scholarship in the last generation is memory and how it shapes historiography. Cloyd's contribution to the field is the first to focus exclusively on Civil War prisons. This thought-provoking book demonstrates how the passions of the postwar fight over treatment of prisoners complicated the process of reconciliation. In the present, as the Lost Cause mythology has stubbornly held on, how we want to remember the war extends to the need for both sides to cast blame on the other when it comes to prisoners of war.

Flags fly over the monument
at the Water Authority building
to commemorate north and
south. (cm)

About the Author

A native of the Finger Lakes of New York, Derek Maxfield grew up 35 miles from Elmira. Today, he is an associate professor of history at Genesee Community College in Batavia, New York. He holds a BA in History from SUNY Cortland, an MA in History from Villanova University, and was a PhD candidate at the University of Buffalo where he is ABD.

In 2013, Maxfield received the SUNY Chancellor's Award for Excellence in Scholarship and Creative Activities for his work coordinating the college's programs related to the Civil War sesquicentennial. More recently, SUNY honored him with the 2019 Chancellor's Award for Excellence in Teaching.

When he is not at the college, he is probably haunting a local cemetery or working on his family tree with a cat in his lap.